The African Social Situation
Crucial Factors of Development and Transformation

The African Social Challenges series:

No. 1: Understanding Africa's Food Problems:
Social Policy Perspectives

No. 2: The African Social Situation:
Crucial Factors of Development and Transformation

No. 3: Social Determinants of Labour Productivity
in West Africa

No. 4: Social Development in Africa:
Strategies, Policies and Programmes after the Lagos Plan

The African Social Situation:
Crucial Factors of Development and Transformation

Published for the

African Centre for Applied Research
and Training in Social Development
(ACARTSOD)

HANS ZELL PUBLISHERS
London • Melbourne • Munich • New York • 1990

Hans Zell Publishers
An imprint of Bowker-Saur Ltd, a Reed International Books Company.
Borough Green, Sevenoaks, Kent, England TN15 8PH

Published for the African Centre for Applied Research andTraining in Social Development (ACARTSOD), PO Box 80606, Tripoli, Libyan Arab Jamahiriya.

British Library Cataloguing in Publication Data

The African social situation : crucial factors of development and transformation. - (ACARTSOD monograph series. African social challenges; no. 2)
    1. Africa. Social conditions, 1945-
    I. African Centre for Applied Research and Training in Social Development
    960.32

ISBN 0-905450-78-7

Library of Congress Cataloging-in-Publication Data
The African social situation : crucial issues facing contemporary Africa.
    221pp. -- (ACARTSOD monograph series. African social challenges : no. 2)
    ISBN 0-905450-78-7
    1. Africa--Social conditions--1960- I. African Centre for Applied Research and Training in Social Development. II. Series: ACARTSOD monograph series. African social challenges : 2.
    HN773.5.A32   1990
    306'.096--dc20   90-43037
                                                      CIP

Cover design by Robin Caira
Printed on acid-free paper.
Typeset by Kat & Mouse Typesetting, St. Clement's, Oxford
Printed and bound in Great Britain by Bookcraft Ltd., Midsomer Norton, nr Bath

Contents

Foreword 1
    ADEBAYO ADEDEJI

1 Introduction 4
    ADEBAYO ADEDEJI

2 The African Social Situation: Major Elements 18
    ERIC P. KIBUKA

3 Approaches to Social Development 47
    AUSTIN N. ISAMAH

4 Social Participation and the Culture of Production: Africa
    between Pastoralists and Cultivators 66
    ALI A. MAZRUI

5 Breaking the Vicious Circle: Refugees and Other Displaced
    Persons in Africa 92
    BARBARA E. HARRELL-BOND

    Appendix 144

6 Women: The Gender Factor in the African Social
  Situation 155
  FILOMINA CHIOMA STEADY

7 Demographic Factors, Labour Supply and Employment in
  Africa. 200
  SEYOUM G. SELASSIE

List of Contributors 214

Foreword

Contemporary problems of underdevelopment in Africa demand that top priority be given to social development issues. There is an urgent need to identify viable options to accelerate the pace of development in this field, taking into account the specific human, cultural, and ecological conditions prevailing on the continent. The need to establish a specialised organ to deal with these and related problems was recognised by the United Nations Economic Commission for Africa (UNECA), which took the initiative of recommending the establishment of the African Centre for Applied Research and Training in Social Development (ACARTSOD).

Resolution 195(XIII) endorsing the establishment of ACARTSOD was adopted by the UNECA Conference of Ministers at its 191st meeting on 28 February 1977. This decision was endorsed in June 1977 at the 14th session of the Organisation of African Unity (OAU) Assembly of Heads of State and Government. The Centre became operational in 1980, with headquarters in Tripoli, Socialist People's Libyan Arab Jamahiriya. The Centre's main objectives include original research focusing on the identification and analysis of social development problems; the organisation of training seminars and workshops at national, sub-regional, and regional levels; the communication of the results of these activities to African governments to assist them in the formulation and implementation of social development policies and programmes; and the dissemination of research findings and publications to universities and other institutions of higher education.

In accordance with its mandate, ACARTSOD has so far produced two major categories of publications: the Research Series, which consists of studies dealing with critical social problems in Africa; and the Training Series, which comprises proceedings of seminars and other pedagogical material. The Centre has now taken another initiative by inaugurating the *African Social Challenges* Monograph Series. Publications in the series are derived from research undertaken by ACARTSOD Senior Social Development Research Fellows, commissioned research, proceedings of the annual regional workshops organised by the Centre at its headquarters, and from the best of the unsolicited manuscripts submitted to ACARTSOD by independent scholars and addressing major social development problems in Africa. Each monograph in the series is intended to have an impact on the resolution of social development problems in Africa by producing practical recommendations for action.

Africa is experiencing severe social and economic crises that threaten to rend the very fabric of society. The *African Social Challenges* Monograph Series has been established in response to these crises, and offers a contribution to the debate on how to ensure that African economies and societies are put firmly on the path to recovery and transformation. Africa must at all costs avoid a systemic breakdown by vigorously pursuing policies and programmes that will bring about transformation, increase its productive base and capacity, and promote societal cohesion and social change.

Contributing to this process is an enormous task, and ACARTSOD needs the full support of its member states, the inspiration and active participation of the intellectual community in Africa and elsewhere, and the guidance of the Governing Council and specialised bodies.

On behalf of the ACARTSOD Governing Board I would like to express my appreciation and gratitude to all ACARTSOD member states, and in particular to the People's

Libyan Arab Jamahiriya, for the financial and moral support they have committed to the Centre. Their continued support will be fundamental to the Centre's ability to sustain the *African Social Challenges* Monograph Series in the future.

Professor Adebayo Adedeji
UN Under-Secretary General
Executive Secretary, UNECA
Chairman, ACARTSOD Governing Board

1 Introduction

Adebayo Adedeji

It is appropriate that the African Centre for Applied Research and Training in Social Development (ACARTSOD) should organize an important regional workshop on 'The African Social Situation' in 1988 - the year of the 30th anniversary of the Economic Commission for Africa (ECA) and the Silver Jubilee of the Organization of African Unity (OAU), the two organizations that gave birth to the Centre.[1] African member states have not only celebrated both anniversaries with appropriate pomp and pageantry, but also have rightly used these occasions to reflect on the difficult question of where we go from here. After the serious and intensive searching of the last few years, it has become clear to all Africans that we must rededicate ourselves to the genuine socio-economic transformation of our continent. Nothing less can get us out of the social and economic quagmire in which we have been floundering.

It is also clear to us all that the social dimension of Africa's development and transformation is as crucial as the purely economic dimension. However, the concepts and ramifications of genuine social development have not always been clearly understood and many a country has relegated social development to a secondary place and allocated only minimal resources to it. It is essential that ACARTSOD, eminent scholars and experts should join the vanguard in the search for a deeper understanding of the social dimension of African development and in the articulation of effective policies, programmes and measures to tackle accumulated social problems.

Through a brief survey of our past and present social conditions I will share some thoughts about the challenges facing our continent. While I will stress the social issues I must emphasize the need for us to take a *holistic* view of our development problematic. We must strive to integrate the economic, political, cultural, technological as well as the sociological dimensions in our analyses and prescriptions if they are to serve any useful purpose. In the final analysis, what we need are strategic thinking and an overall design for our present and future development, in which micro- and macro-economic, social, political, cultural and technological policies and programmes are engineered, combined and implemented *as an organic and dynamic whole, by our people for their own benefit.*

Thirty years ago, at the dawn of the political independence of most African countries, the continent was not engulfed in the multiple crises that threaten to paralyse it today. Indeed, the mood of the early 1960s was one of hope and promise, high expectations and confident assertions about our abilities to take control of the affairs of our emerging nation-states. Our national flags flew high and proudly. They still fly high and we should be thankful and proud of that. But beneath the flags today, the faces of the masses of our people, our children, youth and rural women display acute stresses and frustrations borne out of hunger, unemployment, ill-health and manifold misery. What went wrong with our development, and with social development in particular?

We must not delude ourselves that there are easy solutions to the current social malaise. If we are to understand the African condition, we must have a long historical perspective. That condition does not have recent origins and it was not merely the result of the mature colonialism of the first half of this century. The experience of our forebears, with whom the Europeans first established contact more than 400 years ago, became a most traumatic one. Generations of Africans witnessed the horrific open trade of their kith and kin into slavery; they experienced the shock of European conquest and endured the humiliation of colonialism. This heavy burden of history has threatened our societies with near anomie. Despite the heroic efforts of kingdoms, empires and communities in all parts of Africa to resist the European onslaught, the victory of colonialism ensured that our own social standards and values, traditional knowledge and experience would not apply in most of the areas of socio-economic development that mattered. The historical processes that culminated in colonialism engendered a certain sense of helplessness and lack of self-confidence among our peoples. There were tremendous discontinuities in our value systems, organizations and institutions, and organic changes were brutally interrupted. However, I say 'near anomie' because I am convinced that the African spirit was never broken by the European intrusion. Admittedly, we received a difficult and unenviable socio-economic and political inheritance from colonial rule; but we have maintained enough of our cultural values and humanism to enable us to infuse development with our own uniqueness. The question is, are we willing and ready, academics, development experts, politicians, students, farmers, workers, men and women alike, to try to understand our experience more deeply and to make the right choice to develop the continent with our own resources and for our own benefit?

The present African nation-states emerged from colonial rule with a crushing burden of underdevelopment. Nigeria, the country with the largest economy in the entire region, is a case in point. At independence in 1960, the per caput income of nearly 50 million Nigerians was only 40 Naira. Only about 2.5 million children were enrolled in primary schools and less than three persons in ten of school age and over could read and write. There were about 1,000 registered Nigerian doctors and less than 20,000 hospital beds for the entire population (Adedeji, 1985). Nigeria's levels of social services and facilities, together with those of a few other countries like Ghana and Uganda at their own independence - miserably low as they were - were considered quite remarkable at the time. At independence most countries had far less. Zaire, for example, was left without a single African doctor, lawyer or engineer, and we know only too well the astonishing and painful burden of underdevelopment left by the Portuguese as late as 1975 in our five lusophone African countries.

As Europeans dominated every field requiring modern knowledge, scientific, technical and managerial skills, the education and, of course, general development of Africans was a deliberately slow process. At the end of the 1950s, only 3 per cent of secondary school-aged children were enrolled as pupils in sub-Saharan Africa, compared with 20 per cent in India and 25 per cent in the Philippines. The sub-Saharan region produced only 8,000 secondary school graduates per year and 40 per cent of these came from Ghana and Nigeria. Less than 10,000 students were registered at universities at home and abroad. Other indicators confirmed the extent of colonial social neglect. In 1960 there was just one physician for every 50,000 people in the sub-Saharan region, and these were inevitably located in the administrative capitals, mining towns and port cities - the nodes of the colonial power structure. Government health facilities for rural populations were virtually non-existent. It is no wonder, then, that life expectancy at the dawn of independence was a mere 39 years, the crude death rate a high 25 per 1,000, and children between the ages of one and four perished at the rate of 38 per 1,000 in sub-Saharan Africa compared with 19-23 per 1,000 for their age-mates in other developing regions, and only 1 per 1,000 in the industrialized countries (World Bank, 1981).

It is important to understand that these basic indicators of the social situation were embedded in an economy that was backward in the extreme, an economy dominated more than 50 per cent - and in some cases up to 65 per cent - by agriculture, which had a monocultural structure and used outmoded techniques. It was an economy sharply divided between the 'traditional' and 'modern' sectors with the latter unabashedly under foreign control. Infrastructural facilities were woefully inadequate and primarily served the needs of the export-oriented economy rather than facilitating the transportation of people or the integration of different regions of a country. The political system that circumscribed this fragile economy was an authoritarian and undemocratic one. It operated in a balkanized collection of small colonial territories whose frontiers cut across natural ecological and production zones as well as ethnic groups with common historical origins. The maintenance and development of such policies depended *par excellence* on external factor inputs: labour, capital, equipment and institutions.

I have delineated the background to our situation because it is from there that we can appreciate first, the remarkable progress our countries made during the first two decades or so of independence; secondly, the enormous, deep-rooted and complex nature of our current problems; and, thirdly, the difficult road we must tread from here.

Visible improvements in our social conditions were made through the valiant efforts of the people and the newly independent African states from the 1960s onward. Between 1960 and 1975 regional per caput GDP rose by some 40 per cent. Education became one of the hallmarks of progress, and total school enrolment grew faster in sub-Saharan Africa from 1960 than in any other developing region. From 1960 to 1976 the annual average growth-rates for all educational levels were 6.2 per cent compared with 5.9 per cent for Latin America and 4.2 per cent for Asia. The primary school population increased from 36 to 63 per cent of the total age group; the secondary school population from 3 to 13 per cent; and university students from virtually nil to 1 per cent.

By 1980 the respective ratios were 70 per cent, 14 per cent and 1.8 per cent for the whole continent (ibid.; ECA, 1977, 1983). This was a unique achievement. African governments demonstrated their commitment to education by allocating 20 to 30 per cent of their national budgets to it, and from 1975 to 1980 the continent's per caput educational expenditure rose from US$18 to US$41 (ECA, 1987).

Other social indicators vindicated these efforts. Life expectancy rose from 39 to 47 between 1960 and 1979 and the infant mortality rate fell from 38 to 25 per 1,000 in sub-Saharan Africa. For some 19 low- and middle-income countries, the ratio of population to physician improved from 32,000 in 1965 to 23,000 in 1981; and that of population to nurse from 4,200 to 2,400 in the same period (Akeredolu-Ale, 1988). Progress in the areas of mother and child health, clean water-supply, housing, environmental sanitation and control of endemic diseases was also considerable.

Nevertheless, the pace and quality of these social changes were seriously compromised by the fundamental distortions and structural imbalances in the socio-economic order that had been created almost two centuries beforehand. Social changes were thus directed first and foremostly towards the urban population that constituted less than 20 per cent of the total. There were imbalances in the distribution of social services and amenities within different parts of the same country, with men favoured over women, urban centres over rural communities, and rich over poor. Education and training were urban-centred, whereas the production base was rural. Although agriculture constituted the backbone of the economy, the educational system was not geared towards its improvement nor were the educated orientated toward seeking employment in that sector. For the educated youth, all roads led to the towns, especially the administrative capital, whose white-collar jobs seemed to be the ultimate reward of learning. Cities grew by leaps and bounds, not as a result of industrial and economic expansion but by natural increase and migration from the rural areas.

In 1960, there were only three African cities with populations of over 500,000; in 1980 there were 28. In the first half of this decade, 35 major cities increased at such a rate that their populations were scheduled to double every nine years: the African continent is being forced to urbanize and house more people in towns, and within a much shorter time-span, than Europe or the United States of America had to accomodate during their entire period of urbanization, which spanned several centuries (ECA, 1988). The result is the terrible overcrowding and the housing crisis that is so pressingly evident in most of our cities today.

It is likely that distorted social development would have continued unchanged for a number of years but for important developments in the three major variables of demography, climate and the external economic environment. The impact on our social and economic life of negative changes in these variables since the mid-1970s is so well-known that I will not belabour it here. Suffice it to say that these changes have been a contributory factor in the rapid erosion of the gains of the early post-independence period and in the grim and deteriorating social situation of the 1980s. The crises so created have threatened our very survival, deepened our dependency and shaken our self-confidence, if not our self-esteem.

While there were moderate declines in Africa's mortality rates from the 1960s, fertility levels have remained high with the result that the population has increased at an average annual rate of 3 per cent this century - and this rate is more than double that of current increases in agricultural output. Whereas in 1967-70 Africa achieved a food self-sufficiency ratio of 102, this dropped to 75 in 1978-82, and after the great drought disaster of 1983-5, 25 per cent of our people had to depend on food imports and food aid for survival (Adedeji, 1986; ECA, 1986). The combination of fast-growing population and agricultural decline has contributed to a high level of rural underemployment, accentuated rural-urban migration and lowered productivity throughout the continent. Furthermore, persistent drought and associated desertification have not only devastated our fertile lands, but have also imposed immense stresses on our social fabric, displacing 10 million people and their livestock and adding to the refugee problem. At the height of the drought emergency in 1984, over 1 million people died and 35 million faced famine, malnutrition and debilitating diseases in 24 affected countries. Forty-three per cent of children under five years of age throughout the continent suffered from malnutrition, and 26 per cent of the total African population was undernourished. We will have to deal with the pernicious effects of such malnutrition for years to come. Today we have the highest death-rate in the world for children under five years old, reaching as high as 250-300 per 1,000 live births in places. Debilitating and endemic diseases such as malaria, yellow fever, cholera and yaws, which had been eliminated or largely brought under control in the 1960s and 1970s, have re-emerged. Our life expectancy, though improving, is still only an unenviable 50 years.

The institutional and financial resources of African governments have been insufficient to meet the huge social challenges of the 1980s, and have also been seriously constrained by economic recession, external indebtedness and debt-servicing burdens. The continent's debt-servicing obligation grew from 12 per cent of its export earnings in 1977 to 30 per cent in 1985 and might reach 45 per cent in 1990, whereas 10 per cent or less is considered a healthy benchmark. The social implications of the debt crisis are stark. Health expenditure in many countries fell by over 25 per cent and per caput social expenditure by more than 50 per cent between 1980 and 1986. This regression can be demonstrated by the fact that in 1984, 40 per cent of school-aged children did not attend school, while the figure had been 30 per cent in 1980. Many public educational institutions lack textbooks and equipment and their teachers are poorly paid. Imports of the usual consumer goods, food and medicines are restricted in many countries and prices are high. Meanwhile, the structural adjustment measures adopted by most African countries are having deleterious effects, especially on the poor, women and children (as analysed in the Khartoum Declaration of March 1988, which adopts a human-focused approach to Africa's recovery and development). Very few countries are in a position to increase investments in the social sector.

There is widespread fear of an imminent systemic breakdown of the social and economic order in our continent. In addition to the signs I have outlined so far, there are many others. They include the effects of apartheid and destabilization, political instability, ethnic conflicts, intolerance and civil strife. They also include the refugee problem. We still harbour half of the world's refugees and it is only our treasured traditional sense of hospitality that has enabled us to give succour to and share what we have with the millions of African brothers and sisters who have been forced out of their homes. But it is a fact that what we are sharing is predominantly poverty. Mass poverty, unemployment and underemployment are the main features that characterize our present rural and urban landscape. In 1980-5, some 70 to 75 Africans out of every 100 were living in poverty; that is, they had insufficient income or exchange entitlements to meet their basic needs for food, clothing, housing, health care, and so on (ibid.; ECA, 1983).

Above all, it is the unemployment, idleness and frustration of our youth that so threaten the future social order. In 1987, 45 per cent of Africa's total population was under 15 years of age. Can we provide suitable educational, health and other social services for them? Does a dependency ratio of 93 not severely limit the capacity of the working population to save and invest in productive activities? In 1950 there were estimated to be 67 million youth (i.e., those between 15 and 34 years old); in 1980 there were 141 million and in the year 2025 the projection is 575 million or 36.9 per cent of the total population (Adedeji, 1984). Is this a potential engine of growth or a perennial burden? In 1985, 40 per cent of the labour force, which is growing at the rate of 2.6 per cent per annum, was unemployed or underemployed, and this figure included a high proportion of young university graduates, school-leavers, drop-outs and rural youth. The mismatch between our labour requirements and the output of our educational system has resulted in some 4 to 5 million educated persons being unemployed. Can Africa sustain such a wastage of human resources and social investment?

There are also other kinds of wastage in our society. The growing severity and rising incidence of crime, the spread of violence, corruption, juvenile delinquency and drug trafficking - all have a negative impact on development and the quality of our lives. Although hard data and statistics are inadequate or poorly reported, there are clear indications that the crime problem is assuming increasing proportions in many countries, with serious economic and social consequences. A considerable slice of resources (in terms of labour and finance) have to be diverted from developmental activities to control or prevent crime, treat and rehabilitate offenders and keep law and order. As public institutions fail to maintain law and order, a climate of personal insecurity and fear pervades the lives of ordinary citizens, particularly in our towns and cities. This can hardly be conducive to national growth and development. Crime prevention strategies must be built into planning processes if harmonious development is to be achieved. But a critical factor - and one that must be dealt with - is the decay of a number of social institutions and cultural values that contributes to the rising crime rate. The capacities of basic social institutions and networks such as the extended family have been eroded; the voluntary village and community spirit for participation, development and protection is on the decline; and traditional institutions, arrangements and norms for dealing with certain offences and forms of social deviance have been undermined. A cult of individualism has grown up, associated with the accumulation of political power and wealth, while the tastes and lifestyles of the dominant social classes undermine domestic production as well as traditional values. Meanwhile, modern public institutions established to promote social development through education, health and other social services have proved either inadequate or dysfunctional.

While changes in social and cultural institutions are inevitable as a result of the dynamic development process, some of those changes have been undesirable and have impeded economic and social development. It is important to ask whether such changes could have been avoided by establishing a proper balance in our development strategies between planning and programming for social development and for economic and political development? And now that the problems have emerged, can our anthropologists, sociologists and cultural experts undertake the necessary urgent research to identify ways of halting socio-cultural erosion and reinforcing or creating dynamic popular institutions to support development and promote social cohesion?

These are urgent questions and challenges. Our search for the answers is both an immediate and a long-term task and its results should not be pre-empted. There are, however, four factors that must be taken into consideration. First, a choice has to be made to break with the past and follow a different development path that will be truly self-reliant, transform our societies and serve our interests. Here I refer to the contrasting historical and normative scenarios developed at the ECA secretariat in the 1983 study, *ECA and Africa's Development, 1983-2008: A Preliminary Perspective Study*, which has now been revised as *Beyond Recovery: ECA Revised Perspectives of Africa's Development, 1988-2008*. I am convinced that we must opt for the normative scenario that calls for a fundamental restructuring of our economy and the determination to shake off dependency in all its social, political and cultural forms. The alternative is too grim to contemplate.

Secondly, there is a need for consistency in policies and programmes. In 1980 member states adopted the Lagos Plan of Action (LPA) as the basic framework for radical socio-economic change throughout the continent. In 1985 they adopted Africa's Priority Programme for Economic Recovery, 1986-90 (APPER) in order to focus on a limited number of critical areas in which to lay the foundations for the desired new order. The first critical area is, naturally, agriculture, followed by sectors that *promote* agriculture such as industry, transport and communications, trade and finance, and by concern for drought and desertification and human resource planning, development and utilization. I believe that any reconsideration of our present and future development tasks should take account of and amplify the existing frameworks provided by the LPA and APPER in the 1987 *Abuja Statement on Africa's Economic Recovery and Accelerated Development* and in the 1988 *Khartoum Declaration: Towards a Human-Focused Approach to Socio-Economic Recovery and Development in Africa.*

Thirdly, we should opt for a *holistic* view of development - and this cannot be overemphasised. For far too long economists, planners, scientists, sociologists and development experts have worked separately and at different tempos in our struggle for development. This has sometimes resulted in conflicting sectoral priorities, the disregard of research findings in developmental planning, disjointed national development plans and unnecessary and pernicious sectoral competition. Specifically, economic development should *not* be seen as something apart from the people, and social development must not be viewed as a short-term effort to alleviate the hardships of people outside the framework of production and distribution. Nor should social development be conceived as something that flows automatically from economic growth without the exercise of political will and effective social policies brought to bear on population, education, human resource mobilization, equi-

table distribution of income and other developmental benefits and social justice. To these must be added policies and
programmes to promote cultural values and attitudes conducive to development and societal cohesion.

Fourthly, I think that too many of our people have
inordinate tastes for foreign things and lifestyles. They also
look inordinately to government to provide them with jobs
and meet their basic needs. At the same time, they harbour
a certain distrust of government. Such contradictory attitudes of dependency and suspicion retard growth and do
not make for self-reliant, self-sustaining development. We
must, therefore, rationalize our consumption, define the
parameters of our own political, economic, social and cultural life, generate the factors of our development and, above
all, work hard to make that development beneficial to ourselves.

Finally, Africa's sustainable development requires an
enabling social environment - a social environment that can
stimulate collective problem-solving, self-generated development and self-confidence. Such a social environment
entails the democratization of the development process,
allowing the fullest participation of both sexes and all social
groups in domestic production and equitable consumption.
It implies freedom and de-alienation in the political, cultural
and social spheres and the building-up of a consensus of
values to sustain the rule of law and order, societal peace and
security and to promote the *national* public and civic good, as
opposed to the good of the multitudes of small and large
ethnic groups.

Let us be bold, innovative and practical in our proposals for achieving a new and viable social order for Africa's
development. But let us also be realistic: our real development options are limited; time is running out; and our
people can wait no longer. What should be done *now* and
where do we go from here?

Notes

1 This chapter is based on the opening statement of the workshop, which took place in Tripoli, 26-30 June 1988.

References

Adedeji, A. (1984), 'African Youth and the Challenge of Socio-Economic Development in Africa', convocation address at the University of Zambia, Lusaka, 8 December.

Adedeji, A. (1985) 'Some Reflections on Nigeria's Economic Performance since Independence and Thoughts on Future Prospects', paper presented at the Silver Jubilee Symposium on Reflections on the Development of Nigeria, 1960-1985.

Adedeji, A. (1986), 'Long-Term Development Needs in Africa and United States Response', statement at the Hearing of the Subcommittee on Africa and the Subcommittee on Human Rights and International Organizations of the Committee on Foreign Affairs of the United States Congress, Washington, DC, 7 August.

Akeredolu-Ale, E. O. (1988), 'The Human Situation in Africa Today: A Review' (ECA/ICHD/88/2), paper prepared for the International Conference on the Human Dimension of Africa's Economic Recovery and Development, Khartoum, Sudan, 5-8 March.

ECA (1977), *Preliminary Assessment of Long-Term Development Trends and Prospects in Developing Africa*.

ECA (1983), *ECA and Africa's Development, 1983-2008: A Preliminary Perspective Study*.

ECA/OAU (1986), Africa's Submission to the Special Session of the United Nations General Assembly on Africa's Economic and Social Crisis (OAU/ECA/2XV/Rev. 2, E/ECA/ECM.1/1/Rev. 2).

ECA (1987), *Survey of Economic and Social Conditions, 1985-1986*, pp. 168-9.

ECA (1988), 'The African Social Situation, 1982-1987' (E/ECA/CM. 14/16).

World Bank (1981), *Accelerated Development in Sub-Saharan Africa: An Agenda for Action*, Washington, DC, pp. 9-10 and tables 34, 37-8.

2 The African Social Situation: Major Elements

Eric P. Kibuka

It is evident that problems of poverty, social deprivation and general underdevelopment exist in all the less developed countries (LDCs) of the world. However, because of rapid and frequently unpredictable political changes on the continent, African countries seem to experience these problems with greater intensity than most. The African social situation is consequently characterized by conflict (both within and between different states), pretensions at democracy, a very large number of refugees and displaced persons, the prevalence of curable and preventable diseases, illiteracy, low productive capacities, high population growth-rates, low per caput incomes and therefore poverty, unemployment, intolerable urban social conditions, imbalanced rural-urban growth-rates, very high crime rates and many other undesirable factors.

In this context we shall consider the major elements of the African social situation, which include the population element, the general pattern of social deprivation, the communication gap and deficiencies in the social services sector, with a focus on health, housing, social security, education, land tenure systems and the legal framework. We shall examine the implications of these elements for social development in Africa and identify areas for social policy intervention that is designed to check the rapidly deteriorating social situation. These analyses are preceded by two considerations: first, clarification of the concepts 'social development' and 'social policy', both of which are vital to the analysis of the African social situation; and secondly, a critical appraisal of the broad socio-economic realities of Africa today.

Conceptual Issues

The two significant concepts in the analysis of the African social situation are 'social policy' and 'social development'. It is important that these terms are properly understood, or at least that operational definitions are established for them.

Social Policy

It is assumed that most people have a general conception of 'social policy', which presupposes a degree of enlightenment among the public. However, if these conceptions are applied to specific and practical situations, they often result in distortions of social reality and sometimes outright contradictions. What then is social policy? The first type of definition is one that perceives social policy as 'the study of history, philosophy, sociology and economics of the social services' (Rein, 1970). This definition embraces the traditional view of social services and focuses on the social benefits organized and financed by the majority who are wealthy for the benefit of the minority poor. Such services include housing, health education, services to vulnerable and disadvantaged groups like the physically and mentally handicapped, and other areas of traditional social-work practice. This view of equating social policy with the traditional social services is limiting. In particular, it fails to address such critical sectors as agriculture, land tenure systems, co-operatives and marketing, industrialization and communications. It also omits general questions regarding fundamental freedoms, justice and equity, which directly and/or indirectly have significant impact on any social situation. As these are issues of major importance to the peoples of Africa, it is grossly unrealistic to formulate policies without considering them.

A second, equally restrictive approach to the definition of social policy attempts to separate policy formulation and analysis from the processes of planning, implementation and evaluation (ibid.). This approach draws boundaries between policy, planning, implementation and administration. According to this approach, social policy is defined as 'the simple explication of choices and assumptions underlying present or anticipated programs' (ibid.). The major weakness of this approach is that it avoids considerations of the complex issues of implementation strategies or the possibilities of altering the direction and consequences of policies, or even of making specific and detailed policy and strategic choices.

These attempts to delimit social policy to particular and substantive processes can be very misleading. While the objective may be to enhance clarity, the effect in practice has been to distort reality - all the more so considering that social policy *is both a process and an end in itself,* so that knowledge of both is essential to a full and appropriate comprehension of a social situation: 'It is not the social services alone, but the social purposes and consequences of agricultural, economic, [labour], fiscal, physical development, and welfare policies that form the subject matter of social policy' (ibid.).

It is, therefore, the view here that social policy is a much broader process than that concerned with making deliberate choices, and with the identification, implementation and evaluation of applied solutions. These solutions are deemed to be aimed at improving and enhancing the general welfare and well-being of people and societies. It is this calculated deliberateness that qualifies social policy as 'principles that govern action directed at given ends' (Titmuss, 1974). It can be asserted that one of the major concerns of social policy is to enhance understanding of the implicit rationale and value choices surrounding both the process and substantive issues of social development.

Social Development

Current thinking on development departs substantially from the traditional view that almost exclusively emphasized economic indicators - an approach grounded in modernization theory. It held that the western economic and technological complex is essentially a liberalizing and progressive force, and hence that western societies should provide the model for underdeveloped societies (in this case African countries) to follow. Development is currently conceived as implying positive transformation of society in all spheres of social, economic and political life. The argument is that 'Since the human factor is of decisive importance for increasing the economic efficiency of each society, it is right that the transformation of [humanity, its] behaviour, and. . .socio-productive forces should become the point of concentration of any development strategy' (Van Nieuwenhuijze, 1979).

While economic development may still be concerned with the attainment of concrete quantitative goals in the economic sphere, social development may be defined to refer to the evolution of system capacity for survival within the context of the larger environment of which the social system is a part. Hence, social development represents

> positive changes in individual, group and institutional capacity to place the environment (material resources) at the service of [humanity]. This, among other things, *implies continuous search for the means of ensuring more harmonious and mutually beneficial interactions* among the various units of society in the development, equitable distribution and utilization of natural and [human]-made resources. (ASWEA, 1986; emphasis added)

Without these preconditions, there can be no socio-economic progress and stability.

Accordingly, it is possible to identify two important dimensions of social development that are relevant to our concerns here, namely social development as a process that refers to those aspects of the overall development of society that encompass the harmonization of social relationships, and the developmental preservation of social systems and their values that are likely to promote the positive transformation of society; and social development as a process and product that subsumes all activities intended to bring about an improved quality of life for the general population. The notion of improved quality of life includes improved security and safety of person and property, positive and vigorous social interactions, decent shelter for all, adequate employment opportunities, accessibility to equitably provided basic services, the transformation of the social framework in ways that favour increased social mobility and more effective participation in decision-making processes. These and many other social indicators are considered important components in any social situation, and especially in the African social situation. In particular, they have major implications for the overall development and cohesiveness of society.

To sum up, both social policy and social development must be seen as part and parcel of the same *continuous process* of identifying, formulating and implementing choices with regard to development, choices that reflect equitable distribution and utilization of resources (i.e., social policy) with the ultimate objective of achieving and sustaining the economic, social and political well-being of people (i.e., social development).

Socio-Economic Realities in Africa

Having clarified the concepts of social policy and social development, it is now important to identify some of the main social, economic and political realities and problems in Africa. These represent a generalized picture of the socio-economic situation in this vast and heterogeneous continent. There are obviously many differences, not only among the sovereign states of Africa, but even within each African state. However, given the historical experiences of many of these countries it is possible to identify certain commonly shared features and developmental problems.

We can observe that, since the 1970s, Africa has been faced with a rapidly deteriorating economic, social and political crisis that has varied widely among its member states. These crises, at first sporadic and isolated, have become endemic and pervasive in the 1980s, resulting in the alarming current disruptive situation that is not only devastating lives and property in many parts of the continent, but also promises to become 'a nightmare of total economic collapse, social injustice, human misery and political instability and chaos' (ECA/OAU, 1985). This situation is the product of many complex factors. The colonial (and neocolonial) experiences of African countries left them not only with the immediate source of internal and external hostilities, but also with economies that are still totally dependent on those former colonial powers. After more than 20 years of political independence, African countries, with few exceptions, still find it extremely difficult to free themselves from the state of dependency and underdevelopment in which they were initially left. In their attempts to regain confidence and economic independence, African and other Third World countries demanded a New International Economic Order in 1974. Its promises were, however, found to be illusory (Adedeji, 1983), and African governments realized that the provisions of the New International Economic Order, and other such declarations, were not likely to take them far in dealing with the problems of mass poverty and dependency. Consequently in 1980 the Heads of State and Government of the Organization of African Unity (OAU) adopted the *Lagos Plan of Action for the Economic Development of Africa, 1980-2000*. The major objective of the much publicized Lagos Plan of Action was to reduce or entirely eliminate the dependence of African countries on external sources of food, technology, expertise and lifestyle and to move quickly towards self-sufficiency and self-reliance (OAU, 1981).

The commitment of African governments to the full and systematic implementation of the Lagos Plan has been neither consistent nor satisfactory, and every major social, economic and political indicator continues to describe a deeply depressing situation. These are some of the pertinent facts:

1. The gross national product (GNP) for many African countries has generally declined as a result of many inter-related factors, which include widespread and persistent drought, the extremely hostile international and economic order, the rapidly increasing foreign debt, the archaic and backward means and relations of production, and endless external and internal wars (ECA, 1983).

2. This condition is further compounded by the relatively rapid rate of population growth and the inequitable distribution of resources and opportunities; a per caput income decline resulting in about 70 per cent of the African population being destitute; half the labour force being unemployed or underemployed; the deterioration of the population's health and nutritional status; and educational opportunities being both inadequate and inappropriate for local developmental needs and problems (Ekanemu, 1986).

3. African countries have been characterized by apparently perpetual and pervasive instability. Coups and counter-coups as well as interstate conflicts have been the order of the day. It is also clear that African governments have been unable or simply unwilling to deal decisively with their social, economic and political problems. If anything, they find it easier to blame each other or some distant force for their individual failures. These internal and external conflicts, together with deteriorating socio-economic conditions, have resulted in mass population displacement

and migration and in the unprecedented destruction of lives and property including vital physical structures.

After considering the African condition in fairly general terms, we now turn to the major elements of the African social situation. It should be noted that these elements create situations that frequently lead to internal conflict, political persecution, displacement of large populations and economic stagnation.

The Population Element

There are three components to the population factor that have important implications for the African social situation: high population growth-rates; uneven population distribution; and severe dislocation of normal life through involuntary migration (the refugee question, which is dealt with fully in chapter 5).

In mid-1985 the total population of independent Africa was estimated at about 520 million with an average family size of six or seven children (eight in Kenya; ibid.). The high annual average population growth-rate of about 3.1 per cent is mainly attributed to a lack of knowledge about the implications of population growth by local populations. This is reflected in the broad mix of economic, social and cultural factors that include early age at marriage, the diminishing practices of prolonged breast-feeding and abstinence from sex after childbirth, limited knowledge of modern contraception, the relatively low status of women and the ever-increasing desire for many children in many African cultures. High fertility rates are also attributed to the absence of coherent population policies in many sub-Saharan countries: 'Most African countries have neither formulated nor implemented policies specifically designed to moderate rapid population growth' (ibid.).

Whereas the population growth-rate is estimated at 3.1 per cent, it is estimated that agriculture in sub-Saharan

Africa is unlikely to exceed 2.5 per cent annual growth-rate up to the close of this century (ibid.). Given the fact that agriculture is the backbone of these African countries, this imbalance has major implications for Africa's social situation. Existing high levels of malnutrition are expected to worsen while intensive cultivation of the land is expected to result in a significant increase in the total regional income that is consumed, leading to constraints on the growth of domestic savings necessary for fixed capital formation, an increase in unemployment, and heavy demands on the already over-burdened social service systems, particularly education and health care (ibid.). Creating and maintaining adequate social service systems implies that African governments must divert funds from the much-needed public investments in roads, communications networks, port facilities, industrial water-supplies and other types of infrastructure that help attract both local and foreign private investment. This kind of diversion of investment would have dire consequences for social development in the long term.

Africa's population situation is further compounded by the high proportion of very young people in the overall profile, which in turn increases the dependency burden and affects overall economic performance in the region. When combined with decreasing infant mortality rates, the fact that an estimated 45 per cent of the population is under 14 years of age (about 53 per cent for Kenya) has major implications for the region's consumption patterns, capital formation, indebtedness, labour force and growth of social service systems. A high dependency ratio necessarily results in lower per caput production, since the majority of children contribute to consumption but not significantly to production. This has important implications for the creation of employment opportunities and other aspects of social development. It is, therefore, important that efforts be made to reverse this trend in population growth.

The uneven distribution of population is attributed to unevenly distributed natural resources in the region and high urban growth-rates. The latter factor indicates the absence of concrete rural development policies in most African countries, which in turn renders rural areas very unattractive for large numbers of young people. Urbanization contributes to the decay of rural areas and low agricultural production levels. It is important to note that the refugee question in Africa, which contributes to uneven population distribution, is caused mainly by internal conflicts within member states. The number of refugees in Africa has risen at an alarming rate (Bakwesegha, 1984): in 1965 there were 0.5 million refugees; in 1970 the number rose to 1 million; in 1978 to 4 million; and by 1980 the refugee population was over 5 million. Prolonged drought is also a frequent cause of population displacement, resulting in serious food shortages and exacerbating the already unfavourable food situation across the continent. The refugee situation intensifies famine, increasing the incidence and severity of malnutrition and related diseases as well as causing human mortality, livestock depletion, severe dislocation of normal life and many other undesirable consequences.

The Communication Gap

The communication gap is a major factor in the African social situation, as it has important implications for social development. The concept 'communication' as used here refers specifically to the process of vigorous social interaction through the verbal exchange of views and opinions. A common language spoken by all, therefore, is important for consolidating national ethics and communicating development ideologies.

Within each African country different ethnic groups have different languages, although a few countries have been able to establish national languages, notably Swahili in Tanzania and Kenya and Amharic in Ethiopia. In addition there are the Arabic-speaking countries of North and north-east Africa. For the vast majority of African countries though there are considerable communication difficulties, especially where the majority cannot speak the official national language - be it French, English or Portuguese. These difficulties create problems of social interaction in markets, streets, work-places and many other public places, and are a significant factor in perpetuating differential opportunities in employment, housing, scholarships, etc. It is important to note that at these high levels, the more powerful ethnic groups or nationalities often impose their value systems on the rest of society and frequently take advantage of state machineries, especially the army, the police, the public service and secret security agencies. The lack of any significant commonality, and in particular of a lingua franca, can be considered a cause of conflict and political instability in many African countries and as such as a major impediment to social development. Uganda is a particularly good example of such ethnic diversity where the absence of a lingua franca could be considered a major destabilizing factor. The need for a common national language in every African country, therefore, indicates one important area for policy intervention.

Social Deprivation: The General Pattern

A discussion of the general pattern of social deprivation is important to the understanding of Africa's social situation, and helps to identify areas for policy intervention and social development action. We therefore undertake a brief diagnostic profile of the rural communities where over 80 per cent of Africans still live. The major factors that frustrate the capacities of the masses include poverty, physical debility, vulnerability to 'episodic shocks', the unavailability of essential basic services, and powerlessness (Muzaale, 1986). These five components constitute the deprivation trap. A brief overview of each of them will indicate their implications for political stability, social harmony and overall national prosperity.

Poverty

As a component of deprivation, poverty may be conceived in the context of basic needs, which include nutrition, safe drinking-water, decent and adequate clothing, housing, health care, education, and the opportunity to participate in decision-making processes. The reality in the Third World, particularly in Africa, is that large proportions of the population are undernourished, drink dirty water, live in very poor and unhygienic houses, wear very old or torn clothes, lack access to health care and education services and do not, in most cases, take part in making decisions that effect them directly. This is particularly true for rural areas, although the urban condition differs only in degree. The great majority of urban dwellers live in shanty towns where overcrowding, poor or absent sanitation, public utilities and services, filth and other vices are the order of the day. Similarly, the nutritional levels of the urban poor are hardly any better than those of the rural masses. Health services, although available in the urban areas, are not socially and economically accessible to the urban majority. Underemployment or outright unemployment constitute part of the lifestyle for the urban poor that invariably implies inadequate income.

While most of the population continues to be afflicted by abject poverty, small sections of it enjoy lifestyles comparable to those of the wealthy classes in the developed world: a chauffeur-driven Benz or Volvo, two or three cars for home use, a mansion with servants, and access to scarce and hard-earned foreign exchange for shopping or routine medical check-ups in London, New York or Paris. Of these two contrasting lifestyles the latter suggests that people entrusted with public office and the management of public resources use these facilities for self-aggrandizement rather than for the common good. This obvious abuse of public office, and therefore of public trust, and the plunder and outright mismanagement of public resources in the face of widespread poverty cannot help but breed public distrust, hostility and outright conflict. One of the major reasons why most groups are now seeking access to public office through the use of arms is this desire for self-aggrandizement and self-enrichment, the precedent having been set by those in power.

Physical Debility

Physical debility is the result of poverty. The fact that people are undernourished, drink unsafe water, and live in unsanitary conditions, means that large sections of our populations are still afflicted by debilitating diseases. As these people do not have social and economic access to adequate health care they receive little or no treatment.

Similarly, with inadequate educational facilities, large proportions of our populations remain illiterate and ignorant. This in turn creates a suitable environment for the perpetuation of mutual suspicions and petty quarrels, which weaken the bases of local communities. There are people in the same communities, however, who enjoy easy access to first-class health services, are healthy and physically fit, literate and educated. These few are likely to develop a callous attitude towards the underprivileged or look down upon the disadvantaged majority as primitive, illiterate, backward, and occasionally, as biologically inferior. This situation does not facilitate the growth of social harmony and political stability, but rather is divisive and creates a number of socially and economically distinct groups - the 'haves' and 'have nots'. This fosters disunity at all levels - among different households, clans and tribes or nationalities.

Episodic Shocks

Populations in Africa are also noted for their vulnerability to the 'episodic shocks' that occur frequently in their environ- ments - and particularly in rural areas. Muzaale has used the concept of 'episodic shocks' to refer to all unanticipated and unfavourable severe discontinuities in the conditions of the rural masses (ibid.). Such discontinuities may be the result of natural catastrophies such as drought, flood, epidemics or locust plagues, each of which may lead to crop failure, high livestock mortality, or even destruction of property and massively increased human mortality; and human-insti- gated events such as bush wars, inter-tribal hostilities or traditions that may have effects similar to those of natural events. Rural populations are particularly vulnerable to events of this kind, as they live habitually from hand to mouth and are constantly subjected to pre-harvest hunger. Furthermore, they are defenceless and often have no choice in the location of a bush war in their area. This vulnerability, however, is not confined to rural areas, but is equally char- acteristic of the urban poor, who are subject to frequent and abrupt rent rises, apparently without protection from any authority, the perennial reduction of their purchasing power at the whims of the more powerful business communities, and delayed wage payments without ever any courteous explanation from the powers that be. It is not surprising that when there is a sudden change of government through unconventional methods, looting is considered an appropri- ate response. This kind of behaviour is not spontaneous but rather a calculated expression of latent public hostility and disgust.

Essential Basic Services

The masses do not have access to essential (basic) social services in physical or social terms. In physical terms, the little that there is of medical, educational and marketing services and facilities, including essential consumer goods, tends to be concentrated in national and district capitals. The cost of transportation from rural areas to services in the urban centres often exceeds the cost of the services themselves. Rural isolation is intensified by the fact that many extension workers are absent from rural areas during the wet seasons when their services are needed most. In social terms, many people are denied access to certain services and facilities that may be physically available, as in the urban areas, because they lack the personal contacts so critical to access; extension workers also tend to focus on the so-called progressive farmers who in most cases are in a position to subsidize their cost of living.

The major problem for urban populations is not the physical but the *social* inaccessibility of such services and facilities. The question of personal contacts is vital, the bureaucracy is selectively rigorous and the 'costs' of such services are beyond the economic capacities of most urban dwellers. Thus the majority of the urban population is aware of the presence of certain essential services, but cannot make use of them - a situation that creates enormous resentment.

Powerlessness

Finally, there are few or no opportunities at local level for the majority to participate in decisions and policies that affect them directly. The degree of involvement may be assessed in terms of the institutions or administrative arrangements that are available for enhancing genuine public participation. In most African countries, administrative arrangements are such that they permit only top-to-bottom communication. Policy matters are discussed and decided upon by the top echelons of society and are relayed to the bottom levels expressly for the purpose of implementation. Decisions that are imposed on the people in this way do not take into account their real problems, wishes and aspirations. This common method of managing society on the continent does not aid the development of harmonious and appropriate relationships conducive to peaceful co-existence among the different social groups. In the few countries where attempts have been made to develop upward representational linkages (Person, 1982) - such as the co-operative movement in Ethiopia, the ton-cell system in Tanzania and resistance councils and committees in Uganda - levels of effective functioning have not as yet been attained. These systems are still largely experimental and have had various degrees of success.

The powerlessness of large sectors of the population is mainly a product of the predominance of totalitarian regimes that cannot tolerate power-sharing, with the result that the majority can neither influence the location of social services and facilities nor the prices of their farm products. Their wishes and aspirations, even in matters that are of fundamental importance to them, are simply ignored, perpetuating the rift that exists between rulers and ruled. Urgent intervention is needed at policy level if social deprivation is to be eliminated and social development set securely in motion.

The Social Services Sector

Having previously defined the social services sector as embracing education, the legal framework and social justice, equitable systems of land tenure, health and social welfare, social security, housing and urbanization, we shall now summarise some of the most important features of these components.

The Educational System

It has been observed that the educational system in any country is capable of either sowing seeds of discord or creating positive attitudes toward work, skill and harmony, depending on the rationale underlying it. One great African leader, regarded by some as a philosopher of his time, had this to say about education in his country:

> The educational system introduced into Tanzania was modelled on the British system, but with even *heavier emphasis on subservient attitudes and on white-colour skills*. . . .It emphasized and encouraged the individualistic instincts of mankind [*sic*.], instead of his co-operative instincts. It led to the possession of individual material wealth being the major criterion of social merit and worth. This meant that colonial education induced *attitudes of human inequality*, and in practice underpinned the domination of the weak by the strong, especially in the economic field. (Nyerere, 1968; emphasis added)

This describes precisely the nature of educational systems in many African countries. The introduction of formal education in the early 1900s was originally motivated by the desire to provide 'moral, upright and honest Christian clerks, traders, interpreters and chiefs' (McGregor, 1967) - and this is still so today. A person who successfully attains a high level of education is expected of necessity to enjoy a decent life, assessed in terms of the conspicuous material trappings of success - high office, a very satisfactory wage, attractive house and luxury car, and so on. The equally conspicuous failure of many graduates to achieve this level of affluence can have catastrophic results for a nation.

Most of Africa's educational systems are elitist and encourage individual competitiveness rather than teamwork. A small proportion of parents in Uganda and elsewhere, who belong almost exclusively to the middle- and upper-income brackets and are urban-based, are able to pay for extra evening or weekend classes to coach their children for examinations. But these extra classes do not leave those pupils with time for the acquisition of practical skills such as farming, or for recreation. It is predominantly the children of such able parents who perform well in national examinations and qualify to 'enter strategic professions such as medicine and law' (ibid.). As the history of conflict is one of classes in society, we can concur with McGregor's observation that 'Education for leadership does not always do as much to create a stable society as many of its advocates believe', and we can trace this particular root of conflict back to colonial times.

It can be argued that as our societies are predominantly rural in character, a large proportion of our populations is not yet in a position to take full advantage of elitist systems of education. This can be confirmed by 1983 school enrolment figures, given as percentages of the total age group at each educational level: 57 per cent of children in the appropriate age group attended primary school; 8 per cent attended secondary school, and 1 per cent of those in the 20-24 year age group were in tertiary education (World Bank, 1986). These figures indicate widespread illiteracy and ignorance, which, when combined with poverty can be equated with extreme backwardness. This state of affairs is frequently exploited by the small and fortunate elites who seize the opportunity to misinterpret government policy in their own selfish interests, and to pit one nationality against another. The final product may be national disunity that can erupt on the most trivial and sectarian grounds and lead to conflict. In the presence of widespread illiteracy, we can assume that many millions remain ignorant of their civic rights and obligations, and are unable to make use of simple information relating to innovations in technology and development. These conditions enhance powerlessness in the decision-making process.

The Legal Framework and Social Justice

With such a background of widespread illiteracy, ignorance and backwardness, to what extent does the legal framework in many African countries enhance equality before the law and promote social justice? Given the fact that the legal system is itself dominated by the elite class, is it not likely to be used to defend the interests of this group against those of the majority? Is it not possible that the present legal system is being used to redistribute the control of resources from the poor to those who are already wealthy? These and other related issues have been addressed in a set of observations made by Kabumba, who asserts that the 'legal system, which is very costly to the client, full of legal technicalities, [requires] complex evidence and procedure, is not free from corruption and allows delays in the disposal of cases, is already operating against the poor' (1987). In effect the elitist legal system promotes and protects legalized exploitation and the abuse of human rights and fundamental freedoms. A legal system that is only accessible to the privileged cannot be construed as a people's legal system designed and administered to champion and guarantee their rights and freedoms.

Essentially, the legal systems in many African countries operate solely for the legal counsel, judges and minority rich who can afford to purchase legal services on the open market and pay their way through an often corrupt system. The poor, then, do not enjoy basic human rights and social justice. In spite of economic constraints, African governments should endeavour to review and revise their legal systems and incorporate into them traditional concepts of law and justice, and provide subsidized legal services that are readily accessible to the local majority, especially rural people and the urban poor.

The Land Tenure System

The question of land tenure systems is related to, though quite distinct from, the legal framework issue. Land tenure has not received the attention it deserves in the analysis of the African social situation, yet the significance of this issue rests on the fact that most African economies are based on agriculture and depend on peasant production. Land is a fundamental resource and the peasant relationship with land must be a critical factor in any discussion of the social life of African people.

Peasant-farmer occupation of land is governed by law, traditional customs, litigation or by a combination of these measures. In many traditional societies land was used communally and individuals were free to occupy any unoccupied land, as long as it was not claimed by others. Such arrangements were drastically changed with the advent of colonialism: in effect, communal ownership of land was abolished and boundaries were fixed. Private ownership of land was established, and land was transformed into an economic resource. The introduction of private ownership restricted the geographical mobility of people, particularly in pastoral societies. In some instances the acquisition of land by powerful elites resulted in the dispossession of peasants of the fertile land they needed for subsistence and cultural survival. The acquisition of large tracts of land by entrepreneurs frequently did not stimulate the development of local communities and instead often contributed to rising levels of rural poverty. In some countries, large parcels of land are owned by absentee landlords who continue to hold the peasantry in indebtedness through exactions of rent. In a number of African countries, landlords are able at any time and on any pretext to serve tenants with notice to quit the land. A number of governments have the power to move people from the land whenever it is required for other developments - and in many cases fail to make any arrangements whatsoever for resettling those whom they have dispossessed.

There is, therefore, no doubt that existing land-holding practices are a contributory factor in creating the degree of food insecurity and cash income needs of the vast majority. We need to review and streamline land tenure systems as a matter of priority in order to ensure equitable land-holding arrangements that promote the interests and well-being of *all* the people.

Health Services

The continent's rapidly growing population continues to demand better and more equitably distributed health services and opportunities. Unfortunately, African governments find themselves unable to meet even a small fraction of this demand, with the result that infectious but preventable diseases such as measles, malaria, typhoid fever, and cholera are on the increase. There is widespread malnutrition, along with high infant mortality rates, high child wastage (death before reaching 15 years of age), low life expectancy, problems of pregnancy and many other pathologies. It has been argued that high infant mortality and morbidity rates are the result of communicable diseases and nutritional deficiencies (Makusi and Shao, 1987). Kiwara points out that in the less developed countries (LDCs) more than 10 million of the under-fives have severe malnutrition, 120 million suffer from mild malnutrition and approximately half of all children are undernourished (1983). The situation in Africa is in accordance with this general profile of health in the LDCs. In the absence of adequate health care, debilitating diseases that may otherwise be curable are inadequately treated. The result is a major 'loss to Africa in [labour]-years, in investment and human resources on the one hand, and in human suffering and unfulfilled hopes and expectations on the other' (ECA/OAU, 1985).

It has been argued that Africa's health situation is exacerbated by the relative poverty and underdevelopment of its economies, although we can attribute some of the responsibility to policy-makers who allocate minimal resources to health expenditure in comparison with expenditure on education, industry or defence. The emergence of AIDS (Acquired Immune Deficiency Syndrome) on the continent has aggravated the health situation immeasurably. AIDS has so far claimed, and will continue to claim many lives on our continent (millions of deaths are projected), and yet no effective medical cure or preventive is likely to be available in the near future. AIDS poses major dilemmas for health planners, politicians and indeed the entire population not only in Africa but world-wide. One of the major weapons for controlling the spread of AIDS globally is considered to be a *change in behaviour* - in personal relations, sexual matters and the social value systems and images that are associated with these aspects of life. These changes must take place *at all social levels, from the individual to the national,* but it is extraordinarily difficult to convey to an uneducated person, who may feel perfectly well and appear to be quite healthy, that they are infected with the HIV virus that is likely to kill them in a matter of a few years, and that at the very least they can make choices about not infecting others, who may include their future children. In the light of these very difficult circumstances African governments would be well advised to emphasize the provision of primary health care services for all, using the effective and less expensive community based approaches in addition to the more expensive medical services as structures for dispensing AIDS-related information, advice and prophylactics as well as the more usual types of treatment. Nevertheless, global concern about AIDS, and its incidence in Africa should not obscure the fact that the greatest killer diseases in most African countries are malaria, and water-borne diseases that are related to poor sanitation, lack of clean water and the absence of effective immunization programmes. The prevalence of such diseases is a powerful indictment of the failure of African countries to address some of the key elements of our social situation.

Social Security

The concept of social security has been described as 'a programme of protection provided by society against those contingencies of modern life which threaten the welfare of individuals and which they are not likely to be able to avoid through their own ability or foresight' (ACARTSOD, 1986).

One of the main aims of social security programmes is therefore to ensure consistency and minimize the number and severity of disruptions to an individual's strategies for survival. Sources of disruption may be unemployment, old age, death of a benefactor, work-related injury, maternity or invalidity. A social security system should aim to contain these and other contingencies through the protection afforded by compulsory employer's liability schemes, social insurance, public assistance programmes and the provisions of provident funds or other programmes to which all citizens have automatic entitlement (ibid.). Social security systems in Africa, however, are a preserve of the wage-earning minorities employed mainly in the 'modern' sector of the economy, many of whom are in low-risk occupations and enjoy the many amenities of urban life. At present the social security systems in our societies cater mainly for people who are already in receipt of steady incomes, and do not cover rural people or self-employed urban populations (the informal sector). For these groups, survival is fraught with uncertainty and they increasingly lack traditional guarantees against social risks as a result of a combination of factors that include urbanization and industrialization. Whereas the number of contingencies covered tends to increase more or less rapidly on the one hand, on the other hand the protection extended remains confined to employees, or to some of them (Mouton, 1972).

What this means is that the overwhelming majority of Africa's population is not covered by any form of social security following the breakdown of the traditional mutual-aid systems in the wake of urbanization. There are two reasons for this: social security systems in Africa are not adapted to *African* social and economic needs and circumstances (over 80 per cent of the population live in rural areas with only 20 per cent working in the wage sector), and these systems use methods and means that are in direct 'conflict with the traditional forms of social security prevailing in African societies, especially in the rural and semi-rural areas' (ACARTSOD, 1986). Even where social security cover is provided for wage earners, the bureaucracy and procedures for getting access to benefits are so complicated and frequently corrupt that even the intended beneficiaries seldom enjoy their entitlements under the various systems. Any social policy that aims to provide social security for Africans must take these factors into account. Public education will also be instrumental to its success. As long as people are exploited, and as long as there continue to be no guarantees of continuity in survival strategies in the event of contingencies, there can be no political stability, no harmony and no meaningful social development.

Housing and Urbanization

The final social policy component of the social services sector relates to housing and urbanization. Africa in general and sub-Saharan Africa in particular is undergoing a period of rapid social and economic transformation. One major objective of change is to shake off economic dependence on export crops, and to increase the level of industrialization and consequently achieve acceptable levels of social and economic development. Industrialization, however, leads frequently to rural-urban migration, urban concentrations of workers, their families and relations, and to centralized demands for housing and related urban amenities. It is this centralized demand that leads to housing problems. According to projections by the United Nations Centre for Human Settlements (HABITAT), Africa's urban population is expected to increase massively from 133 millions to 345 millions by the end of the century, in a context of poverty, the threat of famine and global recession (Ndyakina, 1984): the urban housing problem is likely to be with us for a long time. Housing is a socio-political problem that every government and community must continually strive to resolve.

At the time of colonial occupation, towns were merely administrative units inhabited by local people who worked for the European and Asian communities. These two latter groups were considered to be entitled to housing while local indigenous people, though clearly in the majority, were not considered to merit a housing policy. The colonial attitude was that Africans who 'accidentally' had to live in towns should, in spite of their large numbers, be encouraged to live a rural life (Abraham, 1964). Post-independence African governments have yet to form a comprehensive housing policy for urban populations in general, and for low-income earners in particular. This in turn has led to the spontaneous growth of unplanned slum areas in which many dwellings could be regarded as unfit for human habitation. The majority of urban dwellers suffer a significant degree of deprivation and neglect in respect of basic urban amenities and public utilities.

The implications for political stability and social progress are obvious. The urban majority have largely been forced from their rural homes to urban centres by socio-economic forces beyond their control. Most will have left nothing worth calling property: no house, no hereditary land, no land title and no livestock. It is unlikely that these vast urban populations will acquire anything more than a couple of saucepans and a simple charcoal stove. In spite of such extreme deprivation and poverty, these people live in a world where the few are powerful, live in large houses, own fleets of automobiles, have plenty to eat and all those things that symbolize 'development'. In a nutshell, they live in a world of contrasts; a world where abundance co-exists with abject poverty.

For the urban poor, peace carries no promise of getting out of their predicament, whereas conflict and political instability carry the promise of acquiring a house, a car or some other commodity in the course of the confusion. The possession of property, particularly real estate, is vital to the preservation of peace and political stability, and a comprehensive housing policy is therefore an important and urgent requirement in the enhancement of social development.

Conclusions

We have considered the African social situation in general and its major elements in particular. But what lessons do we draw from this analysis? Africa is undergoing a rapidly deteriorating social, economic and political crisis whose underlying factors have been identified as over-dependence on former colonial powers and other external sources for food, technology, expertise, and markets for products; and the rapid population growth-rate.

With respect to the first factor, economic dependency, it is urged that African governments should desist from fighting other people's wars and forge close links among themselves. The formation and continued support of regional organizations such as the Preferential Trade Area (PTA), the Kagara River Basin Organization, the Intergovernmental Authority on Drought and Development (IGADD), ACARTSOD, and many other bodies is a positive step that should facilitate and accelerate social development through co-operation and the sharing of knowledge and facilities for dealing with common problems. It is also recommended that African governments develop and pursue policies aimed at creating broad-based economies capable of sustaining themselves through the use of appropriate local technologies, raw materials and local markets. It is only through these and similar efforts that Africa can hope to improve its social situation radically.

Let us take the second major factor responsible for Africa's unfavourable social situation - the very high population growth-rate. The argument is not that the population of Africa is too large for the geographical space available, but that the 3.1 per cent growth-rate is in excess of the estimated 2.5 per cent growth-rate in agriculture. The dependency burden of about 94 per cent is depressing and implies that Africa must spend most of its revenue and other resources on consumption rather than investment ventures. Effective population control policies and other relevant measures must be initiated to ensure that population growth-rates do not frustrate measures aimed at social and economic development.

Our analysis of the general pattern of social deprivation and discussion of specific components of the social services sector has revealed a very unfavourable social situation for the majority of Africans. African governments must be urged to evolve creative rural development policies and programmes that will provide better standards of living for the continent's 80 per cent majority. Policies and programmes of this kind would also drastically reduce rural-urban migration and reduce the pressure on limited urban amenities. It is also important that creative rural development policies and programmes be supported by realistic, specific social policies in the social service areas discussed here. It is particularly important that governments encourage and promote research into all social issues, individually and co-operatively, at regional and sub-regional levels. Research will provide the reliable data necessary to analyses of the social situation and inform the development of realistic, effective, well-targeted policies and programmes.

It is proposed that African governments should deliberately create the social institutions that permit public participation in decision-making processes in order to realise and sustain social development. This would also stimulate the development of attitudes of self-reliance and accelerate both social and economic development. Finally, these participative processes would have the effect of reducing the opportunities for both the exploitation and suppression of the underprivileged, and political conflict.

References

Abraham, C. (1964), *Man's Struggle for Shelter in an Urbanizing World*, Cambridge, Mass.: MIT Press.

ACARTSOD (1986), *Social Security Systems in Africa*, Research Series 2.

Adedeji, A. (1983), *After Lagos, What?* African Centre for Applied Research and Training in Social Development.

ASWEA (1986), 'Report of the Association for Social Work Education in Africa', 5th Conference, Addis Ababa.

Bakwesegha, C. J. (1984), 'Development Options and the African Refugee Problems', *Africa Refugee Newsletter*, 5.

ECA (1983), *A Survey of Economic and Social Conditions in Africa 1981-1982* (E/ECA/CM.915).

ECA/OAU (1985), *Social Trends and Major Social Development Problems in Africa*.

Ekanemu, I. I. (1986), 'Population Trends and Policies in Africa', paper presented at the ASWEA-IASSW Training Workshop, Nazareth, Ethiopia, 6-20 December.

Kabumba, I. (1987), 'The State of Social Stratification in Uganda: A Critical Assessment', unpublished paper presented at Mawazo Workshop 'The Class Question in Africa', Makerere University, 1-3 May 1983.

Kiwara, A. D. (1983), 'Health Education and the Impact on Socio-Economic Development among the Rural Population', unpublished paper, University of Dar-es-Salaam.

McGregor, G. P. (1967), *King's College Budo: The First Sixty Years*, London: Oxford University Press.

Makusi, G. J. and Shao, I. F. (1987), 'Some Conceptual Aspects of the Under-Development of Health in the Less Developed Countries', unpublished paper.

Mouton, P. (1972), *Social Security in Africa*, ILO.

Muzaale, P. J. (1986), 'Organization and Delivery of Social Services to Rural Areas', unpublished paper presented at the ASWEA/IASSW Training Workshop, Nazareth, 6-20 December.

Ndyakira, A. (1984), 'Housing the Urban Explosion', in *The People Newspaper*, Monday 12 November.

Nyerere, J. K. (1968), *Ujamaa: Essays on Socialism*, London: Oxford University Press.

OAU (1981), *Lagos Plan of Action for the Economic Development of Africa 1980-2000*.

Person, D. S. (1982), 'Alternative Local Organizations Supporting the Agricultural Development of the Poor', in D. Leonard et al., *Institutions of Rural Development for the Poor*, Institute of International Studies, University of Berkeley, California.

Rein, M. (1970), *Social Policy: Issues of Choice and Change*, New

York: Random House.

Titmuss, R. M. (1974), *Social Policy*, London: George Allen and Unwin.

Van Nieuwenhuijze, C. A. O. (1979), *Social Development: Supplement or Corrective to Economic Development?*, The Hague: Institute of Social Studies.

World Bank (1986), *The World Development Report*, New York, p. 329, table 29.

3 Approaches to Social Development

Austin N. Isamah

Every African government can claim to have formulated some plan or policy directed at 'social development', and government officials are usually quite willing to elaborate upon the 'achievements' of these plans and policies. Any discussion of African approaches to social development, if it is to be adequate, must cover all the different strategies adopted by different governments, but for the purposes of this chapter it will be more practicable to classify the different strategies into several broad groups: the economic growth approach, the modernization approach, the African socialism approach and the basic needs approach. While some details may be lost in this exercise, it will, however, underscore the urgency of the need to formulate a comprehensive blueprint for social development that is suited to the unique circumstances of the African continent. The aim here is to evaluate existing approaches paying particular attention to their relative degrees of success or failure.[1]

The point of departure is a definition of 'development' and the place of social development within that framework. Webster's *Third New International Dictionary* defines development as 'the act, process or result of development; the state of being developed; a gradual unfolding by which something . . . is developed; gradual advance or growth through progressive changes'. The word 'develop' is a common element that requires further elaboration, and

Webster's *Dictionary* defines 'develop' as 'to cause to unfold gradually; conduct through a succession of states or changes each of which is preparatory for the next'. Thus development implies the advancement or progression of a phenomenon or entity from one state to another. Applied to concrete societies, the implication is that development involves a gradual (and sometimes not so gradual), change from one form of society to another, possibly a progressive change, although instances of retrogression also occur. In this context development means the progressive change of a society from a lower undifferentiated form to a higher complex form, and it can only be conceived in a historical context.

Development implies total change involving *all* spheres of society. This qualification is necessary in view of the prevailing and unfortunate trend to reduce all development effort to the economic sphere. Although development *qua* development is a very broad phenomenon that affects all spheres of human society, economic development involves changes only in the modes of production of societal goods and services, and although economic development can influence development in other spheres, this is not usually the case. As Development Dialogue (1972) has argued, the development of a society is *social* development, a process in which 'economic' and 'non-economic' elements interact organically with each other. Attempts to isolate economic development are therefore unscientific. Development thus defined is a multivariate process of quantitative and qualitative change that may not be measurable in the short term or cardinally.

Experience in Africa, however, has consistently shown that development is not conceptualized in this all-inclusive manner. The preoccupation with economic development has meant the relative neglect of other spheres of development and has relegated the social development objective to the background. This is a grave omission for, as ACARTSOD suggests, social development makes *people* the focus of the development effort and seeks to develop their potentialities in a total sense. It embraces programmes and activities that should enhance the capabilities of all members of society to adequately fulfil existing and changing social roles and expectations, and accomplish the various goals that they have set for themselves. Furthermore, to the extent that this has meant the absence of concrete measures addressed specifically to social development objectives, it has also adversely affected the performance of African economies and the quality of social and political processes. In particular it has undermined the life-chances and objective quality of life of all the less powerful (non-elite) groups in society. The major argument here, therefore, is that hardly any systematic social development approach has emerged from Africa. The plans, policies, and declarations that do exist cannot be differentiated from existing economic development models, which share the basic assumption that social development will automatically follow in the wake of economic development. The danger in the very close interweaving of social development strategies with economic development models is that the failure of the latter also means failure of the former. Thus it is not surprising that Africa has neither developed economically nor socially. We will now conduct a brief evaluation of social development approaches.

The Economic Growth Approach

This approach to social development was the dominant one in Africa, especially during the colonial era, and it can be argued that all subsequent approaches have been derived from it. It is usual for African scholars, in writing about the colonial experience, to over-romanticize the situation in pre-colonial African societies. Though it is difficult to speak of social development in the modern sense with regard to pre-colonial societies, certain features of it can be considered here.

The pursuit of material well-being was embedded in social and community life. In this sense the economy functioned primarily as a by-product of family kinship, political and religious obligations. The institutions through which goods were produced and distributed were embedded in social institutions. Land and labour, the dominant factors of productive activity were not treated as commodities to be bought and sold. They were allocated usually in accordance with kinship, political or tribal rights and obligations. It is a social right to receive land and necessary inputs to produce. Distribution of goods and services was in the form of obligatory gift-giving between kin and friends and obligatory payments to political and religious authorities.

But social development in 'traditional' pre-colonial societies did not depend solely on economic growth, which became the case during the colonial era. Unemployment, housing, food, skill acquisition, etc., which are contemporary social problems, were given appropriate solutions within the family and relations network. The sick, the disabled, famine and drought were managed by community, political and religious institutions. Most of these features of the traditional society did not survive colonialism.

The colonial enterprise itself was undertaken for purely economic reasons: to obtain cheap raw materials and slaves; to find markets for cheap manufactured goods; and to find areas for the investment of surplus capital. This economic mission was undertaken in several ways. First, formerly disparate but small socio-economic and political entities were combined into larger political entities that became states at independence. Secondly, governance of the emergent political entities passed from traditional forms of authority into the hands of alien administrators with equally alien ideas of government. Thirdly, the traditional basis of economic activity was undermined by the dual processes of proletarianization and peasantization, with an increasing urban bias. Fourthly, social life came to be predicated, not on the strength of community solidarity, but on the basis of membership of a society characterized by the increasing predominance of specialized groups. Finally, social development (without which humanity vegetates) became problematic and, therefore, needed to be dealt with on a societal level.

The colonial governments, and some governments in contemporary Africa who subscribe to this approach, came to see social development as incidental to economic growth, which may be defined 'as a rapid and sustained rise in real per capita output and attendant shifts in the technological, economic and demographic characteristics of a society'. This was clearly apparent in colonial society where any degree of social development was incidental to the colonial economic mission. Thus a few educational institutions were established here and there to provide enough literate Africans to keep the economy moving; along with a few health establishments to keep workers and miners healthy enough to work, and minimal housing arrangements designed solely to keep labour within the reach of capital. Roads, railways and harbours were constructed to aid colonial economic growth and wherever no economic gain stood to be made, no form of social development took place. Hardiman and Midgley (1982) argue that this approach adopted by planners of developing countries was based on the historical experience of western nations that, largely because of industrialization, experienced rapid economic growth and attained a high level of social welfare. As a result, they argue further, the majority of developing nations initiated development plans that concentrated on economic growth policies and expected them to raise incomes and improve standards of living and welfare. The implication is that economic planning that aims to raise incomes through rapid economic growth assumes that individuals and their families will have the means to meet their own social needs as well as satisfy their economic wants, leaving outstanding social problems such as crime, delinquency, prostitution and so on to state agencies. The economic growth approach to social development has largely failed to 'deliver the goods', and this is evident even where some economic growth has occurred. According to Seidman (1974):

> The inadequacy of national plans in Africa becomes particularly evident when evaluated in terms of this development perspective. Several countries have achieved significant increases in per capita income: but these benefits have more often than not been concentrated in a few urban centres with modern office buildings just over the skyline, sleek automobiles crowd the streets, and the wealthy few live in luxurious villas furnished with refrigerators, air conditioners, television sets and innumerable servants. The vast majority of the population continue to live in the rural areas in thatched-roofed homes with dirt floors, scratching a bare living from lateritic soils with little more than hoes, their average life expectancy about thirty to thirty-five years. Hundreds of thousands of eager younger men and women flee the countryside annually, hoping to share some of the conspicuous advantages of 20th century life in the cities - but many of them are condemned to live in squalid urban slums, taking any job for wages as low as $15 or $20 a month, or joining the growing ranks of unemployed who sometimes number as much as 20-30 per cent of the urban labour force.

Nobody can quarrel with the desire of governments to achieve economic growth through concentrating on export production of either agricultural raw materials or minerals as a means of raising real output per caput and generating greater surpluses to be reinvested in more export production and consumption of goods. But it is surprising that some countries still stick to this strategy of linking social development to economic development, even in the face of all the consequent dysfunctions for society at large.

The Modernization Approach

The modernization approach is similar to the economic growth approach, although it does not regard development

as a one-sided, isolated phenomenon. In fact the modernization thesis was applied widely after World War II and was
intended primarily as a device to distinguish between the
'developed' countries of western Europe, North America,
the Soviet Union and Japan and the 'developing' nations of
Africa, Asia and Latin America. Modernization theory is
highly multidisciplinary and eclectic, incorporating the
anthropological theory of acculturation, Talcott Parson's
theories of action and social change, notions of the plural
society derived from Furnival, and political science theory
on the evolution of nationalism. These strands were inter-
preted through a particular view of change that was essentially dualistic and regarded 'tradition' and 'modernity' as
opposed forces, the latter growing at the expense of the
former. This dichotomous perspective is perhaps best exemplified by Talcott Parson's pattern variables, a formulation
that in turn owes much to Ferdinand Tonnies' distinction
between *Gemeinschaft'* and *'Gesselschaft'*. When applied to
concrete societies, the following series of attitudinal and
behavioural patterns, which are mutually opposed, are held
to be characteristic of 'traditional' (or pre-industrial) and
'modern' (industrial) societies.

Pattern variable and social change
Traditional society
1. Affectivity: immediate gratification, expressiveness in
   actions, relationships.
2. Collectivism: priority given to collective goals.
3. Particularism: duty owed on the basis of kinship membership and collectivity.
4. Ascription: status ascribed by 'who you are'.
5. Diffuseness of role.

Modern society
1. Affective neutrality: deferred gratification, an instrumental approach to work, relationships.
2. Individualism: priority given to individuals.

3. Universalism: duty owed to all; (bureaucratically) equal treatment.
4. Achievement: status acquired by 'what you have done'.
5. Role specificity: separation of work from leisure and community roles.

The value-laden assumption underlying this concept of social change sees the traditional as basically 'irrational' and as such undesirable in contemporary circumstances, and regards modernity as 'progressive' (Smelser, 1963). Thus, all contemporary societies are expected to undergo a more or less unilineal progression from traditionalism to modernism. Though scholars are not agreed as to the nature of modernism, there appears to be a consensus as to what constitutes modernity. Among the salient characteristics (operational values) of modernity are:

1. A degree of self-sustaining growth in the economy - or at least growth sufficient to increase both production and consumption regularly.
2. A measure of public participation in the polity - or at least democratic representation in defining and choosing policy alternatives.
3. A diffusion of secular-rational norms in the culture - understood approximately in Weberian-Parsonian terms.
4. An increment of mobility in society - understood as personal freedom of physical, social and psychic movement.
5. A corresponding transformation in the model personality that equips individuals to function effectively in a social order that operates according to the foregoing characteristics (*Encyclopedia*, 1968).

Translated into concrete reality, modernization, in historical terms, is the process of increasing 'structural differentiation', a process by which more specialized and more autonomous social units are established. This is seen to occur in several different spheres: in the economy, the family, political systems and religious institutions. The developing countries of Africa, Asia and Latin America are currently undergoing a process of structural differentiation, whereas the societies of Europe, North America and Japan are already modern and thus provide an example of what the future of developing societies would look like. In this respect Eisenstadt (1966) saw modernization as:

> historically the process of change towards those types of social, economic and political systems that have developed in West Europe and North America from the 17th Century to the 19th Century and then have spread to other European countries and in the 19th Century and 20th Century to the South American, Asian and African continents.

Similarly, Moore (1963) suggests that modernization is 'a total transformation of a traditional or pre-modern society into the types of technology and associated social organizations that characterize the advanced economically prosperous and relatively politically stable nations of the Western world'. Two factors make the modernization thesis very significant for this discussion; first, the emphasis on economic development, which takes place through:

1. The modernization of technology leading to a change from simple traditionalized techniques to the applications of scientific knowledge.
2. The commercialization of agriculture, which is characterized by the move from subsistence to commercial farming leading to specialization in cash crop production and the development of wage labour.
3. Industrialization, which displaces animal power with machine power.
4. Urbanization, which comprises changes to ecological dimensions and the movement from farm and village towards large, growing urban centres.

Hand in hand with the emphasis on the economic aspects of development is a concomitant emphasis on the role of the individual in the modernization process - and this is a most significant factor. The transition from traditionalism to modernity requires that certain attitudes, expectations and behaviour patterns are inculcated into the individual:

> Modernization produces the societal environment in which rising output per head is effectively incorporated. For effective incorporation, the heads that produce (and consume) rising output must understand and accept the new rules of the game deeply enough to improve their own behaviour and to diffuse it throughout the society. (Lerner)

The social development approach implicit in modernization arises from the urgent need for the individual to *learn* these 'new rules of the economic growth game'. This was to be achieved primarily through the expansion of the educational system in developing countries. Mabogunje (1980) captures this phenomenon accurately.

> Investment in education, or more broadly in human resources, came to be seen as a major and critical basis of societal change. Indeed, in many countries a new epithet 'social' came to be added to development, to counter the previously almost synonymous association with economic development.

Development as modernization saw a new concentration in many developing countries on the building of schools and colleges and expanding enrolment figures at all educational levels, as well as on adult education, wider mass media coverage, particularly through radio and television, more health centres and medical establishments, and the provision of improved housing and recreation facilities. Without doubt these are commendable objectives, which would have transformed the African continent had they been achieved. In reality, however, the situation was considerably different.

> This form of development was, however less critical of content than of form. In a situation of changing social conditions, it continued to educate, to inform and to minister to health needs through processes reminiscent of the period of colonial tutelage or procedures borrowed directly from the advanced industrial countries. (Ibid.)

One important dysfunction of this social development approach has been that it heightened the social expectations and aspirations of individuals, most of which it can neither attain nor fulfil. Furthermore, it exacerbated the income disparity between a small group of 'modernized' Africans and the larger majority of citizens and between rural and urban areas. The main point, however, is that many African countries have pursued social development policies and strategies under the broad concept of modernization with various degrees of success.

African Socialism

If modernization can be criticised as Eurocentric, the African socialism approach was developed as an 'indigenous alternative'. African socialism is, however, a catch-all term for a wide range of ideas that all claim some affinity with socialism. It is possible, as Kraus has argued, to study socialism (or for that matter capitalism) in terms of several distinct, but generally interrelated dimensions that embody certain social and economic relationships: first, as a mode of economic production and distribution that entails certain economic and social relations and usually gives rise to a limited range of probable political relationships; secondly, as a more or less integrated political belief system or ideology; and thirdly, as certain policies and programmes. In Africa, socialism has been used predominantly as an ideology, and ideological statements by leaders are readily accessible and easier to evaluate than actual political beliefs or behaviour.

As an ideology, socialism in Africa 'seeks to create an identity that can transcend tribal and communal boundaries' that stand in the way of development. Bell distinguishes between two variants of African socialism - the North African and the sub-Saharan. The North African type was fashioned largely by French-educated native intellectuals and assumed a revolutionary hue, particularly in the late 1950s, through vigorous independence movements against France, for example in Algeria and to a lesser extent Tunisia. In the popular imagination, however, African socialism is primarily associated with sub-Saharan Africa and with names like Nkrumah, Senghor, Touré and Nyerere. The problem is that 'African socialism', which developed in the late 1960s, meant different things to different individuals, depending on the contemporary and historical environmental. Yet some common ground can be identified. First, there is the acceptance that economic productivity must be enhanced. As Arrighi and Saul (1973) noted 'Professed African socialists are, to be sure, uniformly interested in economic development; they have also sensed that some form of co-ordinated expansion on the agricultural and industrial fronts is required in order to attain that goal.' Thus, most African countries committed to the idea of socialism assign to government the priority function of 'exercising the primary responsibility for accumulating capital'. This primacy accorded to government removes or ought to remove the possibility of exploitation, a feature characteristic of the capitalist strategy being repudiated. The primacy ascribed to production in the socialist approach is perhaps best illustrated by Nyerere's concept of *Ujamaa*. *Ujamaa* is consciously designed as a socialism of production, for low production is perceived as a more urgent problem for Tanzania than any other. According to Nyerere (1968): 'Tanu is involved in a war against poverty and oppression in our country; the struggle is aimed at moving the people of Tanzania (and the people of Africa as a whole) from a state of poverty to a state of prosperity.'

In addition to the general recognition of the place of enhanced production, the second general feature of African socialism is its African origins, a concept Nyerere calls 'African humanism'. Most proponents of this approach stress the indigenous character of communal land owner-ship, the egalitarian nature of society and the extensive network of social obligations that ties clans together. Thus the major component of this brand of socialism is the notion of African 'familyhood' or communalism. With reference to *Ujamaa*, Nyerere (1969) argues that:

> *Ujamaa*, then, or 'familyhood' describes our socialism. It is opposed to capitalism, which seeks to build a happy society on the basis of exploitation of man by man; and it is equally opposed to Doctrinaire Socialism which seeks to build its happy society on a philosophy of inevitable conflict between man and man.

The social development approach in African socialism is thus one that has to be welfare-oriented. Senghor (1964) in his book *African Socialism* stated that in keeping with the ordering of priorities, Senegal had earmarked a substantial part of its budget for 'social development' by which he meant health and hygiene, municipal administration, hous-ing and education. Also emphasised is the democratic proc-ess inherent in the development strategy. By this it is meant that the participation of the masses is required not only in increasing production but also in the distribution of benefits. Again, as in the modernization approach, the results for those countries espousing African socialism as a social development strategy have varied nationally, though an outstanding success is yet to be recorded on the continent. In fact, when measured against six key elements identified by Sweezy (1972), the success or failure of this approach is brought out in greater relief. These key elements, towards which any socialist strategy must make significant progress are:

1. Equality both materially and in terms of status.
2. Workers' participation in management and management's participation in work.
3. Complete freedom of discussion and criticism.
4. The achievement of combining agriculture and industry and breaking down urban conglomerates.
5. Treating work as life's most creative activity.
6. Ending the system whereby the earning and spending of incomes is the key mechanism for the distribution of goods.

It is evident that any society that can attain these ends would have attained complete social development. However, experience shows that African countries subscribing to the African socialism development strategy are yet to achieve much success.

The Basic Needs Approach

The basic needs approach to social development arose out of the World Bank's 'rediscovery of poverty' in the 1960s. This came with the realization, after more than a decade of development planning, that economic growth had been of no significant benefit to the vast majority of citizens. According to Adelman and Taft (1973): 'Hundreds of millions of desperately poor people throughout the world have been hurt rather than helped. Their destinies become a major and explicit focus of development policy in the 1970s and 1980s', and economic development may have served merely to promote social injustice. Similarly, McNamara, the former President of the World Bank, stated:

> Increases in national income - essential as they are - will not benefit the poor unless they reach the poor. They have not

reached the poor to any significant degree in most developing countries in the past, and this is in spite of historically unprecedented average rates of growth thoughout the sixties.

This realization of the increasing impoverishment of the majority of citizens in the developing world ushered in a new era of international agency involvement in poverty alleviation. Especially noteworthy is the World Bank's 'Redistribution with Growth' strategy. All the strategies and plans adopted by development-oriented international and national agencies can be classified as the basic needs approach. It must be noted, however, that the International Labour Organization (ILO) has been in the forefront of this struggle with its World Employment Programme, which more than any other articulates the basic needs approach. What does the basic needs approach imply? The ILO summarizes this in *Basic Needs in Danger* (1982):

The basic needs approach is a reminder of one of the most fundamental objectives of development: to provide every human being with the opportunities for the full physical, mental and social development of his or her personality. It represents an advance from the previous abstract economic development approaches to the concrete, from the general to the specific and from the aggregations to the identification of vulnerable groups in society. It includes and identifies the needs of special groups, such as children below school age, lactating and child-bearing [women], people in distant regions, recent young migrants to cities and the old, the disabled, the sick - i.e., those who are not just unemployed but unemployable. The specific list of basic needs to be satisfied . . .includes food, nutrition, safe water, shelter, health, education, transport, energy, a range of simple goods, such as clothing and household goods, and people's participation in the development process. Employment, including self employment, is one of the most important basic needs as it is both an end and means to the satisfaction of various household consumption needs.

It is evident that the basic needs approach constitutes the most adequate and the most comprehensive approach to social development yet formulated. Perhaps more important, however, is the fact that, in addition to seeking to fulfil the necessary needs of the populace, it also calls for their participation. It is argued that the 'Mass commitment and mobilization that would appear to be essential in most countries to basic needs targets within a reasonable period can only be forthcoming in a system involving mass participation and support.' The successful implementation of this approach will have a regenerative effect on the economies and general life-situations in developing societies:

> High and growing inequality of income generates rapidly increased demand for luxury goods (in particular, expensive consumer durables) but relatively sluggish growth of effective demand for basic foodstuffs and consumer goods. Increased productive employment and higher incomes for the poor will change both the level and rate of growth of demand for basic consumer goods and public services. This shift in the composition of demand should induce a shift in the pattern of production towards goods which in many cases are more suitable for production on a relatively small scale. (ILO, 1977)

This may tend to generate higher levels of productive employment to the extent that the new output mix is characterized by greater labour intensity. Moreover, the new conditions should increase the incentive to search for and use more appropriate technologies.

There is no question that the various agencies involved have done their utmost to implement the basic needs approach successfully, and much material and human effort has gone into this endeavour. Although this approach has produced a few sporadic successes, the general social situation on the continent remains dismal.

Conclusion

The limited success of the basic needs approach does not imply that the problems in Africa are intractable. Perhaps it demonstrates that African problems can best be solved by Africans themselves. On the other hand, the relative failure of the other social development approaches implemented by African governments also suggests that there are certain fundamental obstacles to overcome throughout the continent if any meaningful social development is to occur. These obstacles include:

1. A defective understanding of the character of development and of underdevelopment.
2. The growth 'fetish', or a naive obsession with this as society's ultimate goal.
3. The misunderstanding and distortion of the social development function, and especially a gross underestimation of its instrumental role in the development process.
4. A chronic conservatism that has crystallized into pathological fear and suspicion of all innovative and critical ideas and tendencies.
5. The lack of a long-term vision or perspective.
6. The defective moral-normative values of the policy-making class, which include materialism, individualism and elitism.

These are daunting obstacles that could frustrate even the most concerted efforts, but they are not an excuse to admit defeat. Social scientists, enlightened developmentalists and others, in Africa and elsewhere, must pool resources and work together to overcome these obstacles and inaugurate a truly African approach to social development that is comprehensive, dynamic and capable of extricating the continent from its present social and economic malaise.

Notes

[1] Prof. Akeredolu-Ale's unpublished paper, 'Social Development in Nigeria', which he presented to the Lagos State Government, Ministry of Economic Planning in 1985, is used as a general reference source throughout this chapter.

References

Adelman, I. and Taft, C. T. (1973), *Economic Growth and Social Equity in Developing Countries*, Stanford: Stanford University Press.

Arrighi, G. and Saul, J. (1973), *Essays on the Political Economy of Africa*, New York: Monthly Review Press.

Brookfield, H. (1975), *Interdependent Development*, London: Methuen.

Chers, A. (1980), 'Work and Values, Shifting Patterns in Industrial Society', *International Social Science Journal*, XXXII, 3.

Clark, W. E. (1978), *Socialist Development and Public Investment in Tanzania, 1964-1973*, University of Toronto Press.

Crowder, Michael (1982), *West Africa under Colonial Rules*, Evanston, Illinois: North Western University Press.

Development Dialogue (1972) *Towards a Theory of Rural Development. Development Reconsidered*, 2.

Eisenstadt, S. N. (1966), *Modernization: Protest and Change*, Englewood Cliffs, New Jersey: Prentice Hall.

Encyclopedia of the Social Sciences (1968), vols 10, 13-14.

Fadayomi, T. O. (1987), 'Social Development Strategies, Policies and Programmes in West Africa in the Light of the Lagos Plan of Action', unpublished report.

Hardiman, M. and Midgley, J. (1982), *The Social Dimension of Development: Social Policy and Planning in the Third World*, New York: John Wiley and Sons.

ILO (1977), *Employment, Growth and Basic Needs: A One World Problem*, Geneva: ILO.

ILO (1982), *Basic Needs in Danger*, Addis Ababa.

Long, N. (1977), *An Introduction to the Sociology of Rural Development*, London: Tavistock.

Mabogunje, A. L. (1980), *The Development Process: A Spatial Perspective*, London: Hutchinson University Library.

Moore, W. E. (1963), *Social Change*, Englewood Cliffs, New Jersey: Prentice Hall.

Nyerere, J. K. (1968), *Freedom and Socialism*, Oxford University Press.

Nyerere, J. K. (1969), *Freedom and Unity*, Oxford University Press.

Seidman, Ann (1974), *Planning for Development in Sub-Saharan Africa*, New York: Praeger.

Senghor, L. S. (1964), *On African Socialism*, London: Pall Mall.

Smelser, N. J. (1963), 'Mechanism of Change and Adjustment to Change', in B. F. Hoselltz and W. E. Moore (eds), *Industrialization and Society*, The Hague: Mouton, in collaboration with UNESCO.

Weber, M. (1984), *Theory of Social and Economic Organisation*, New York: Oxford University Press (provides an excellent discussion of the concept of 'rationality').

4 Social Participation and the Culture of Production: Africa between Pastoralists and Cultivators

Ali A. Mazrui

Three civilizations have failed to solve Africa's crisis of underdevelopment. The civilizations are indigenous, Islamic and western cultures. Together they constitute Africa's triple heritage.

One area of interaction among the three legacies concerns the balance between people, pasture and production. The human population in Africa is the fastest growing of any region in the world. Although the percentage of pastoralists in Africa is a small minority of the total number of people, that percentage is over 40 per cent of the pastoralists of the world. Among communities in Africa most devastated by drought are those that are partly dependent on livestock. Both thirst and hunger have often decimated these groups.

Underlying the whole situation is an important divide in Africa between cultures with an almost religious preoccupation with animals and cultures with ancestral fascination with land. The divide has played a major role in creating the ecological context of the twin crises of water and food. Let us turn to this cultural divide more fully as part of the background to the twin crises of water and food in the postcolonial era.

Lovers of Land and Lovers of Animals

There are of course various groups in post-colonial Africa that are inspired by the cattle imperative, often resulting in major disputes with others and in actual military confrontations of the ancient 'tribal' kind. Groups whose behaviour has caused headaches among policy-makers in modern African capitals include not only the Maasai but also the Turkana of Kenya, the Karimojong of Uganda and the Barabeg of Tanzania. However, cattle raising may no longer be the paramount concern. Overgrazing is reaching crisis proportions. From the point of view of our concerns with the triple heritage, there is an additional factor of remarkable cultural relevance among these groups of pastoralists and herders. On balance they are among the most resistant to western influences, and sometimes also to Islamic influences, unless the impact is sustained over a long period of time.

The rural world of Africa is, in fact, divided between lovers of land and lovers of animals. Lovers of land in this context are those Africans who have responded to the challenge of cultivation and agriculture, and have learnt to take advantage of the soil and seeds as a means of production. These are the Africans who plant, tend their farms, and harvest their corn and yams. Lovers of animals, on the other hand, are those Africans whose entire way of life is bound by a cattle complex or a camel imperative, or a concern for sheep and goats. Land is important to these Africans, but primarily for the sake of pasture for their beasts. Nor do they necessarily cultivate the pasture. They accept it as nature's bounty, very much as ancient gatherers accepted wild fruit and wild roots.

When I was an undergraduate in England we used to debate the question of whether the entire world was divided between Aristotelians, who are pragmatic, and Platonists, who are idealists - the rhetoric of debate at British universities is sometimes influenced by the heritage of the classics in

European civilization! In fact the issues that were being thrashed out were sometimes of universal significance. We might, therefore, ask whether pastoralists and herders of Africa like the Maasai are, in the ultimate analysis, Platonists. They certainly *idealize* their cattle to such an extent that they often resist the lure of possible profit for selling them, and sometimes even the temptation to kill them for food. Pastoralists of this kind in Africa are often fanatical idealists in relation to their animals, with a world view that is resistant to empirical forces of change, and which romanticizes their beasts.

African cultivators and agriculturalists - the lovers of land - are more like Aristotelians, empirical and pragmatic in many of their attitudes. On balance it has been more the cultivators and agriculturalists who have responded to commercialization of rural production and to the price mechanism as an inducement for certain forms of production. Many of these Africans were soon influenced by the colonial order to enter into cash crops rather than food production, and cultivate cotton, sisal, coffee and tea for export in response to the lure of the new cash economy.

The most striking illustration of pastoralists on one side and cultivators on the other is perhaps the impressive proximity between the Maasai of Kenya and their neighbours, the Kikuyu. For centuries the two groups have lived close together, sometimes fought each other and sometimes intermarried. The Maasai have remained primarily people of cattle, fanatically pastoralist. The Kikuyu have, for centuries, been cultivators. Then came the west in the form of white settlers and administrators at the turn of this century, and settled near both groups. The agricultural Kikuyu before long responded to the new economy and the new culture that had come with the European settlers. Although the Kikuyu interest in cultivating cash crops was sabotaged by the latter out of fear of economic competition, there was no doubt about a Kikuyu response to the temptations of money-making and the inducements of the profit motive.

Culturally, the Kikuyu also responded dramatically to the new forms of education that had come with the missionaries and the whole new universe of western civilization. During the colonial period, the Kikuyu even initiated their own independent schools, in the face of inadequate facilities provided by the colonial order. Even after independence the *Harambee* schools of Kenya, based on local self-reliance in erecting the building and raising money for the teachers, have been in part a continuation of Kikuyu initiatives during the colonial period and their response to both the new western economy and the new western culture.

In striking contrast, their pastoralist neighbours - the Maasai - maintained during the colonial period an obstinate cultural distance from both the new capitalism and the glamour of cultural westernization. The Maasai have walked tall and often semi-naked, ferociously possessive of their cattle, and indifferent to the new culture of western suits and ties, western hats and even western shoes. Not for the Maasai the cash crops or the obsession with earning foreign exchange. These herders have sometimes been such deep idealists about their animals that rather than sell them when faced with drought and inadequate pasture, they have let them grow thinner and then die. One of the great problems of cattle societies in Africa is this reluctance to sell animals even when faced with their probable death. After all, a man does not sell his children even if he sees them starving to death, so why should he sell his cattle? What is more, the reluctance to sell, and the cultural obsession with maximizing one's herd, have often resulted in overgrazing and caused crises of starvation and death.

On a purely pragmatic basis, one of the solutions to the crisis of famine in Africa is the commercialization of cattle breeding and the lifestyles of cattle societies like the Maasai and the Turkana. Attempts have been made to influence these groups in the direction of responding to selective capitalism and the profit motive, engendering some economic value for the cattle instead of almost pure cultural value. However, most efforts towards replacing a cattle culture with a cattle economy have so far failed. The pastoral Platonists have remained defiantly idealistic in their attachment to both their ancestors and their animals. In recent times one casualty has been the land - impoverished by overgrazing, defenceless against the vagaries of the weather.

Between Capitalism and Statism

As for the lovers of land in post-colonial Africa, they have tended to be the true heirs of the imperial Raj in most countries. Unlike the hard-core pastoralists, the cultures of cultivation responded more clearly to the stimulus of both western capitalism and the western ideology of statism. Both capitalism and statism - when transplanted to Africa - have played havoc with the political economy and food production.

In both pastoralist and agricultural cultures before colonial rule, sacredness was not reserved for the human species. It was not just human beings who were created in the image of God. The whole universe was in the Almighty's image - star by star, creature by creature, tree by tree. There was a traditional cultural respect for the ecology. Some rocks were sacred; some trees were left alone precisely because they were profane. The baobab tree in many African cultures enjoyed the protection of being 'haunted'.

Then Islam came. Suddenly a thoroughgoing monotheism made it difficult to share sacredness with rocks and clouds. At least Islam did allow for 'sheitans' and 'genies'. Even though Islam did not have sacred animals, it did have one or two profane ones. The ecology and the animal world still retained some moral standing - a shield of ethical protection.

Then came the west and its *secular* impact. Many of the ancient taboos that protected the environment were eroded. The world of wild animals was stripped of its misery and sacred restrictions. The forest ceased to be the abode of ancestors. The baobab tree was ready to be stripped for commercial advantage. The rape of the ecology was no longer sacrilegious. Capitalism had arrived. And with it came new forms of deforestation and the despoiling of the environment.

Some African societies before colonial rule did not even have a money economy. Surplus acquisitiveness was still culturally alien. Subsistence was for a while not merely an economic necessity; it was a preferred way of life. That was one reason why the imperial powers initially found it so hard to persuade Africans to be employed for wages - instead of working on their own 'tribal' farms. But with the arrival of the money economy and the profit motive, Africans are now in quest of surplus. Commercial deforestation, poaching of endangered species, and corruption in high places have taken their toll.

Lovers of land among Africans have also inherited the western sub-ideology of *statism*. A preoccupation with the paramountcy and prestige of the state has sometimes delayed announcements of impending drought or famine. A preoccupation with maintaining the inherited territorial boundaries of the colonial order has sometimes made famine worse - and famine-relief hazardous. Statism in Africa has been mother of tyranny and war, while capitalism has been father of greed and corruption. If capitalism and statism are posing such problems in production, is socialism the way out? Let us look at this alternative more carefully.

Socialism: Good Climate, Bad Soil

As a generalization, we might say that the intellectual climate for socialism in Africa is quite good, though the sociological and material soil is not fertile enough for socialism. Let us explore this twin proposition more fully.

The reasons why the intellectual climate for socialism in Africa is good include basic historical continuities and discontinuities. For one thing, many Africans from both pastoral and agricultural cultures have come to associate capitalism with imperialism conceptually. In reality, you can have socialism accompanied by imperialism - and the Chinese can soon equip you with the necessary vocabulary concerning 'social imperialism' and 'Soviet hegemony'. It is also possible to be a capitalist country without being an imperialist country - Switzerland and Finland might be considered by some as good illustrations of non-imperialist capitalism. In Africa's historical experience, however, it is indeed true that modern capitalism came with imperialism. The enemy of imperialism is nationalism; the enemy of capitalism is socialism. If there is indeed an alliance between capitalism and imperialism, why should there not be an alliance between African nationalism and socialism? Such a paradigm of intellectual and ideological convergence has been found attractive in many parts of Africa, though it is more manifest among lovers of land than lovers of animals.

A second consideration that has contributed to the favourable intellectual climate for socialism in Africa concerns the whole accumulation of frustrations with efforts to develop Africa through western patterns of economic growth. Many Africans are seeking alternative strategies of social and economic improvement out of a sheer sense of desperation at the inadequacies of the first decades of independence. African pastoralists especially have suffered in this period. In reality, socialist experiments in post-colonial Africa so far have yet to yield any greater improvement for the masses than other experiments. On the contrary, sometimes the social costs of socialism in Africa have indeed been rather high. It is arguable that while there are relatively successful petty capitalist experiments in places like Kenya, Malawi, Tunisia, and the Ivory Coast, socialist Africa has yet to produce a significant improvement in the material conditions within which the masses live. The nearest socialist success story is perhaps Algeria - and that needed the sale of oil to the capitalist world to buttress it, and has since cracked under the pressures of the international oil glut. In spite of these contradictions, however, many Africans are so disenchanted with the first two decades of independence that they would not mind experimenting with socialist approaches to social transformation.

The third factor that predisposes many Africans in favour of socialism is the rampant corruption among the immediate post-colonial rulers of the continent, all the way from Egypt to Zimbabwe before the implementation of socialism. Again, corruption is by no means a peculiarity of capitalism, as many of those who have travelled in socialist countries will testify without necessarily having lived in those countries. However, there is no doubt that social discipline can, at times, be more difficult to uphold in conditions of laissez-faire economic behaviour than in conditions of relatively centralized planning and supervision. On balance, it is indeed arguable that the socialist ethic is, almost by definition, more opposed to 'kick-backs, good will bribery', and even profit itself, than the ethic of acquisitive individualism.

The fourth factor that has contributed to the favourable intellectual climate for socialism in Africa is the widespread belief that traditional African culture, among both pastoralists and cultivators, was basically collectivist, and 'therefore' socialist. We are all familiar by now with claims by such leaders as Nyerere and Mboya to the effect that the morality of sharing in traditional Africa, the ethic of responsibility for the young, the old, and the disabled, the imperative of collective ethnic welfare, were essentially a distributive ethic akin to socialism. Pastoralist Africa was, in addition, exceptionally *egalitarian* - and egalitarianism is one of the foundations of socialism.

Because of this broadly favourable intellectual climate, most African governments soon after independence paid some kind of lip-service to socialism. Even regimes like that of Jomo Kenyatta and Léopold Senghor managed to adopt, in the initial years of independence, a partially socialist rhetoric, although love of land was often too strong to permit socialist land reform. Kenya's love of land soon created large plantation owners, replacing the colonial settlers.

Regimes that planned to go the route of the one-party state were, nevertheless, tantalized by socialist symbolism. After all, the presumed centralizing tendencies of socialism could help justify a one-party monopoly of power. Prospects for socialism in the first decade of African independence did seem to be congenial. Nasser, Nkrumah, Sekou Touré, Julius Nyerere and Boumédienne were seen as architects of a new socialist Africa. What then went wrong? This is what brings us to the barrenness of the sociological soil, in spite of the favourable intellectual climate. One entrenched sociological factor was simply the primacy of ethnicity in Africa as against class consciousness. Among both lovers of land and lovers of animals, most Africans are members of their ethnic group first and members of a particular social class second. When the chips are down, Ibo peasants are more likely to identify with the Ibo bourgeoisie than they are with fellow peasants in Yorubaland. Somali pastoralists are members of their clan first and foremost. Jaramogi Oginga Odinga in Kenya attempted to form a radical socialist party for land reform. He soon discovered that his supporters were almost exclusively Luo. Chief Obafemi Awolowo invoked socialist rhetoric in both the First and the Second Republics of Nigeria. He soon discovered that he was a hero not of the disadvantaged classes of Nigeria as a whole, but of both privileged and suffering classes of Yorubaland. On balance, it can be argued legitimately that whenever there has been a neat confrontation and competition between the forces of ethnicity on one side and the forces of class consciousness on the other side, ethnicity has almost invariably triumphed in Africa among both pastoralists and cultivators. This is one primary factor underlying the infertility of the sociological soil for an ideology like socialism.

A related factor is the strength of elites in Africa as against social classes as such. The new elites, especially, have emerged out of the womb of western imperial acculturation. Cultivators have been particularly responsive to western culture. It has not been the possession of wealth necessarily that opened the doors to influence and power, but initially the possession of western education and verbal skills. Pastoralists were slow to go to school, but Africa's lovers of land soon became lovers of learning. The initial political establishment of post-colonial Africa was dispro-portionately comprised of a westernized and semi-western-ized core. This galaxy of westernized stars has included names like Nkrumah, Nyerere, Senghor, Kaunda, Ferhat Abbas, Obote, Houphouet-Boigny, Banda, Bourgiba, Mug-abe, Nkomo, Sadiq el-Mahdi, Machel, Neto, and others. This created a basic sociological ambivalence on the African scene. On the one hand, it seemed that the most opposed to imperialism rhetorically, and the ones most likely to link it to capitalism, were precisely the elites produced by the west's cultural imperialism in Africa. Even when these elements became truly revolutionary, there was a basic contradiction. After all, Karl Marx had expected the most revolutionary class to be the least advantaged class in the most advanced societies. This was deemed to be the prole-tariat in industrial western society. When we look at revolu-tionary leaders in Algeria, Angola, Tanzania, Sekou Touré's Guinea, however, and examine the western credentials of the leaders, you may be inclined to conclude that the most revolutionary of all classes in those societies were the best advantaged. In other words, westernized Third World radi-cals were the most likely to produce the dream of socialist transformation. Therefore it is not the least advantaged social class in the most advanced society (the proletariat in the west), but the best advantaged social group in the least advanced societies (the westernized bourgeoisie in Third World countries) who are the true agents of revolution in the last quarter of the twentieth century.

Yet lovers of land were also inclined to be lovers of new ideologies. It is indeed a socio-linguistic impossibility for an African to be a sophisticated Marxist without being, at the same time, substantially westernized. This is partly because the process of becoming a sophisticated Marxist requires considerable exposure to Marxist literature, both primary and secondary. Access to that literature for the time being is only minimally possible through indigenous African languages like Kiswahili, or Yoruba, or Amharic. Even in Arabic, Marxist literature is relatively limited. An African who wants to read many of the works of Marx, Engels and Lenin must have been substantially initiated into the literary culture of the west. Pastoralists from among the Fulani or the Maasai or even the Somali are less well represented in this group than those of agricultural societies. Even Africans who go to China or the Soviet Union need to have been previously Europeanized. Scholarships to China and the Soviet Union are not normally offered to rural rustics untouched by western schools or their equivalents. The nature of elite formation in Africa can, therefore, be counted definitely as an aspect of the non-congenial sociological soil that socialism has to confront in African conditions.

A third factor of this barrenness of the soil for socialism concerns Africa's organizational capabilities in the present historical phase. Many hastily assume that a tradition of collectivism in a traditional setting is a relevant preparation for organized collective efforts in a modern setting. Some even assume that the egalitarianism of pastoral Africa can be used as an organizational resource for modern socialism. Unfortunately, much of the evidence points the other way. Collective effort and pastoral equality based on custom and tradition and kinship ties tend to leave Africa unprepared for the kind of organized collectivism that needs to be based on command rather than ritual. If socialism requires a rational, efficient command structure that is not based on custom, ethnic empathy or ritual, the present stage of social change in the African experience is still inhospitable to socialist transformation.

The fourth aspect of the infertility of Africa's sociological soil would take us back to issues of historical continuity.

Many African economies have already been deeply integrated into a world economy dominated by the west. Even some of the pastoral societies are feeling the force of commercialized animal husbandry. African countries that go socialist domestically find that they are still integrated in the world capitalist system. The rules of that system are overwhelmingly derived from principles evolved in the history of capitalism. In international trade countries seek to maximize their return and acquire profit. The rules of business and exchange at the international level, the banking system that underpins those exchanges, the actual currencies used in money markets and in meeting balances of payments, are all products of the capitalist experience. Countries like Vietnam, Angola, and even Cuba discover soon enough that their best economic salvation is to gain international legitimacy by western standards. Vietnam and Cuba may fail in gaining that legitimacy, but it is part of their ambition to begin receiving western benefaction and to have easy access to western markets for their goods, and western currency markets as well.

Once again what all this means is that Third World countries can make their internal domestic arrangements socialist while remaining deeply integrated in the international capitalist system at the same time. It has also been noted that a country like Tanzania is today more dependent on the world capitalist system than it was before it inaugurated its neo-socialist experiment under the Arusha Declaration in 1967.

Thus this is the configuration of factors that, on one side, reveals that Africa is ready for socialism intellectually and, on the other side, warns us that the material conditions for genuine socialist experimentation in Africa are not yet at hand. The intellectual climate is promising; the sociological soil is forbidding. Africa's lovers of land and lovers of animals are, once again, caught up in the contradictions between cultural continuities and the political economy of change. Economic culture is not merely a matter of policy and ideology. It is often a matter of gender and technology as well. It is to these latter discussions that we must now turn.

The Gender of Social Development

Since the colonial period Africa has witnessed significant changes in the roles and functions of men and women. In both pastoral and agricultural cultures there has been a belief that God made woman the *custodian of fire and water.*[1] In cultivating cultures woman is also in charge of *earth.* God himself took charge of the fourth element of the universe - the omnipresent *air.* Men were in charge of the larger animals, especially among pastoral societies.

Custody of fire entailed responsibility for making energy available. The greatest source of energy in rural Africa is firewood. The African woman became dispropor- tionately responsible for finding and carrying huge bundles of firewood, though quite often it was men who chopped down the big trees initially. Custody of water involved something that was a symbol of both survival and cleanli- ness. The African woman became responsible for ensuring that this critical substance was available for the family. She has trekked long distances to fetch water. However, where a well needed to be dug, it was often the man who did the digging. The custody of earth among lovers of land has been part of a doctrine of *dual fertility.* Woman ensures the *survival of this generation* by maintaining a central role in cultivation - and preserving the fertility of the soil. Woman ensures the *arrival of the next generation* in her role as mother - the fertility of the womb. Dual fertility becomes an aspect of the triple custodial role of African womanhood, though always in partnership with the African man (p'Bitek, 1971).

What has happened to this doctrine of triple custody in the period since 1935? Different elements of the colonial experience affected the roles of men and women in Africa in different ways. Among the factors that increased the woman's role on the land was wage-labour for the men. Faced with an African population reluctant to work for low wages for somebody else, colonial rulers had already experimented with both forced labour and taxation as a way of inducing Africans (especially men) to join the colonial work force. Pastoralists were less affected by these imperial machinations.

According to Margaret Jean Hay, (whose work was among Luo women in Kenya) wage-labour for men took some time before it began to affect women's role on the land.

By 1930 a large number of men had left Kowe at least once for outside employment. . . .More than half of this group stayed away for periods of fifteen years or more. . . .This growing export of labour from the province might be thought to have increased the burden of agricultural work for women. . . .As early as 1910, administrators lamented the fact that Nyanza was becoming the labourpool of the entire colony. . . .Yet the short-term migrants of the 1920's were usually unmarried youths, who played a relatively minor role in the local economy beyond occasional herding and the conquest of cattle in war. Furthemore, the short-term labour migrants could and often did arrange to be away during the slack periods in the agricultural cycle. . . .Thus labour migration in the period before 1930 actually removed little labour from the local economy and did not significantly alter the sexual division of labour. (Hay, 1976; Cutrufelli, 1983)

However, Margaret Hay goes on to demonstrate how the Great Depression and World War II changed the situation, as migrant labour and conscription of males took a larger proportion of men away from the land. This was compounded by the growth of mining industries like the gold mining at Kowe from 1934 onwards:

The long-term absence of men had an impact on the sexual division of labour, with women and children assuming a greater share of agricultural work than ever before. . . .The thirties represent a transition with regard to the sexual division of labour, and it was clearly the women who bore the burden of the transition in rural areas. (Hay, 1976)

Among non-pastoralists, women became more deeply involved as 'custodians of the earth' in this period. In Southern Africa the migrations of men to the mines became even more dramatic. By the 1950s a remarkable bifurcation was taking place in some non-pastoral South African societies - a division between a male proletariat (industrial working class) and a female peasantry. South Africa's regulations against families joining their husbands at the mines exacerbated this tendency towards 'gender-apartheid', the segregation of the sexes. Many women in the Front Line States had to fulfil their triple custodial role of fire, water, and earth in greater isolation than ever. Some of the nomadic tendencies of pastoralists were now affecting the cultivators as well.

The wars of liberation in Southern Africa from the 1960s took their own toll on family stability and traditional sexual division of labour. Some of the fighters did have their wives with them. Indeed, liberation armies like ZANLA and ZIPRA in Zimbabwe and FRELIMO in Mozambique included a number of female fighters. However, on the whole, the impact of the wars was disruptive of family life and of the traditional sexual division of labour.

After independence there were counter-revolutionary wars in some of the Front Line States. The most artificial of the post-colonial wars was that of Mozambique, initiated by the so-called Mozambique National Resistance (MNR or Renamo). The movement was originally created by reactionary white Rhodesians to punish Samora Machel for his support for Robert Mugabe's forces in Zimbabwe. After Zimbabwe's independence the Mozambique National Resistance became a surrogate army for reactionary whites in the Republic of South Africa - committing a variety of acts of sabotage against the fragile post-colonial economy of Mozambique. Again, there have been implications for relations between

the genders. In addition to the usual disruptive consequences of war for the family, by the mid-1980s the MNR
had inflicted such damage on the infrastructure in Mozambique that many migrant workers never got home to their
families in between their contracts with the South African
mines. The miners often remained on the border between
South Africa and Mozambique, waiting for their next opportunity in the mines, without ever having found the transportation to reach their families in distant villages of Mozambique.

Among lovers of land it is not completely clear how
this situation has affected the doctrine of 'dual fertility' in
relation to the role of the cultivating African woman. One
possibility is that the extra long absences of the husbands
have reduced fertility rates in some communities like those
in Mozambique. The other scenario is that the pattern of
migrant labour in Southern Africa generally has initiated a
tendency towards *de facto* polyandry. The woman who is left
behind acquires, over time, a *de facto* extra husband. The two
husbands take their turn over time with the woman. The
migrant labourer from the mines has conjugal priority between mining contracts if he does manage to get to the
village. He also has prior claim to the new babies unless
agreed otherwise. There is no doubt that such arrangements
occur in Mozambique. What is not clear is how widespread
de facto polyandry is becoming in Southern Africa. If the
more widespread pattern is that of declining fertility as a
result of extra long absences of husbands, the principle of
'dual fertility' has reduced the social functions of the fertility
of the womb and increased the woman's involvement in
matters pertaining to the fertility of the soil. On the other
hand, if the more significant tendency in mining communities in Southern Africa is towards *de facto* polyandry, a whole
new nexus of social relationships may be in the making in
Southern Africa (BBC/WETA, 1985-6; Mazrui, 1986). Some
of the cultural tendencies of pastoralists like the Maasai were
now manifest among Southern African agriculturalists.

Other changes in Africa during this period, which affected relationships between men and women, included the impact of new technologies on gender roles. Cultivation with the hoe still left the African woman centrally involved in agriculture. However, cultivation with the tractor was often a prescription for male dominance. The tractor among cultivators was like the bull among cattle herders. Among pastoralists women often handled smaller animals, from chickens to goats. Men handled cattle and controlled the bull. In the new cultivating technology there was a similar division of labour based on scale and complexity.

> When you see a farmer
> on bended knee
> Tilling land
> For the family
> The chances are
> It is a *she*
>
> When you see a tractor
> Passing by
> And the driver
> Waves you 'Hi'
> The chances are
> It is a *he*

Mechanization of agriculture among lovers of land in Africa has tended to marginalize women. Their role as 'custodians of the earth' is threatened by male prerogatives in new and more advanced technologies. It is true that greater male involvement in agriculture could help reduce the heavy burdens of work undertaken by women on the land. On the other hand, there is no reason why this relief in workload for women should not come through better technology. Tractors were not invented solely by men. Were bulls intended to be controlled by men?

Another threat to the central role of African women in the economy in this period has come from the nature of western education. It is true that the westernized African woman is usually more mobile and has more freedom for her own interests than her traditional sister. However, a transition from custodian of fire, water, and earth to keeper of the typewriter is definitely a form of marginalization for African womanhood. Typing is less fundamental for survival than cultivation. The westernized African woman in the second half of the twentieth century has tended to be more free, but less important for African economies than the traditional woman in rural areas.

The third threat to the role of the African woman in this period came with the internationalization of African economies. When economic activity among cultivators was more localized, women had a decisive role in local markets and as traders. However, the colonial and post-colonial tendencies towards enlargement of economic scale have increasingly pushed women to the side in international decision-making. It is true that Nigerian women especially have refused to be completely marginalized, even in international trade. But on the whole, the Africans who deal with international markets and sit on the boards of transnational corporations are overwhelmingly men. At the meetings of the Organization of Petroleum Exporting Countries - where Muslims predominate - there are additional inhibitions about having even Nigeria represented by a female delegate.

What is the future avenue that is likely to change the balance between men and women in public life in Africa? The reasons why women are politically subordinate are not to be sought in economic differentiation. Women in Africa are economically very active; women in Saudi Arabia are economically neutralized, yet in both societies women are politically subordinate. Thus economic differences are not the real explanation of political subjection of womanhood.

What is indeed universal is not the economic role of women, but their military role. Throughout Africa (and, indeed, the world) women are militarily marginalized. What will one day day change the political balance between men and women is when the military machine becomes bisexual. Curiously enough, pastoralist Somali are leading the way. The Somali army has started recruiting women. The Algerian air force has started recruiting women pilots. Both Muslim societies in Africa are beginning to give a military role to women, some of whom are drawn from pastoral traditions. However, the future needs more than tokenism in gender roles. In this continent of coups we may have to wait for the day when the announcement of a coup in West Africa declares as follows: 'Brigadier-General *Janet* Adebiyi has captured power in a military takeover in Lagos.'

Such a gender revolution will of course take several generations to mature - preceded as it is by millennia of masculine specialization in the martial arts among both lovers of land and lovers of animals. What may come sooner to Africa than the gender revolution is the second major shift we have to engineer - a more general transformation of Africa's level of expertise. While the continent may indeed be awaiting both a sexual revolution and a scientific one, prospects for the latter may be more imminent than for the former. Meanwhile traditional roles of women persist. Perhaps the most fundamental for survival are their functions as mothers and their role as custodians of water. Both those areas of activity are caught up in one grossly underestimated crisis in post-colonial Africa - *the crisis of clean water*. Let us turn to this crisis in greater detail.

In Search of Clean Water

Food aid is a familiar enough concept. Water aid may be 'the wave of the future'. Singing (Band Aid) or running (Sport Aid) in order to feed those who are hungry makes good humanitarian sense. Performing for those who are short of clean water is at least as compelling a cause. In reality, far more African children die from lack of clean water than from famine - though the famine is disastrous enough. Indeed, more young Africans die in a single year from diseases linked to contaminated water than are likely to die from AIDS in the rest of the twentieth century. The lack of clean water causes a variety of diseases. These include cholera, bilharzia, different forms of diarrhoea, typhoid - all of them ruthless killers of children and sometimes adults. Malaria's relationship with stagnant water is more complex - but still relevant to infant mortality. Two to three million children in Africa die every year from diarrhoea alone. Malaria claims the lives of an additional million.

A new hazard has entered the scene with increased westernization - bottle feeding. I took my western wife to Kenya for the first time in 1963. She was startled to see a woman relative of mine pouring sand into her baby's feeding bottle. Molly asked the relative in astonishment, 'What are you doing?' The relative answered in puzzlement, 'Well, of course, I am cleaning the baby's bottle!' Molly exclaimed, 'Cleaning with dirty sand?' The idea of using sand from the pathway as a kind of scrubbing soap for a baby's bottle was one of Molly's first culture shocks in Africa. Of course the sand is then washed out and the bottle appears to be 'scrubbed clean'. However, if the water is already contaminated, the risk of polluting the baby's milk increases at each stage. The risk multiplies further when an African mother goes even more 'modern' and uses powdered milk instead of fresh cow's milk. The powder is of course mixed with water. If the water is not clean, the infant's health is in danger - perhaps the infant's life.

Curiously enough, the problem of contaminated water in Africa is part of the population explosion. Precisely because many children are dying, many more children are being born. Birth, death and clean water are interlocked in the demography of Africa. Women as mothers and women as custodians of water are in a state of crisis.

Well-meaning foreigners have often asked me why we permit a population explosion in our continent when we have so many economic problems and so much starvation. The answer lies in this convergence of forces among both lovers of land and lovers of animals. African values do indeed favour the birth of many children; but western skills try to ensure their survival. African traditions promote a high birth-rate; western medicine controls the death-rate. African belief in *ancestors* is being overtaken by the growing number of *descendants*. Indeed, according to African tradition, a person's immortality after being buried depends upon being remembered among the living. To become an ancestor beyond the grave requires having descendants still alive. To put it in modern terms, one can never be completely dead as long as one's genes are part of the living, part of one's children and grandchildren.

> O joy! that in our embers
> Is something that doth live,
> That nature yet remembers
> What was so fugitive!

Thus having children is not only an insurance to protect the parents in old age - it is also a way of safeguarding their immortality. Parents can be remembered as effectively by *two* children as by *seven* - provided the two survive. Although the international effort to save Africa's children has intensified recently, the toll each year is still millions of young casualties. A number of African countries have undertaken nation-wide inoculation of children, and the casualty rate in the villages is declining, but the annual carnage is still devastating. The poignancy of small coffins among the luggage on public transportation in Africa is one of the meeting-points between bereavement and deprivation, between personal pathos and poverty. If immortality depends on one's blood flowing in the veins of the living, bereaved parents suffer a double blow. The funeral of their child is partly a funeral of themselves. The funeral is partly of their own claim to an afterlife as they bury their loved one today. Death in Africa is a many-sided experience - linking the living, the dead and those yet to be born.

In the long run African couples have to be assured that their first babies will survive before they can take the risk of not having any more. The fear of infant mortality continues to affect the dream of parental immortality. Only when African parents begin to bury fewer children will they learn to bear fewer babies. When all is said and done, African mothers do not need sermons about the prevention of further births. They want protection for babies already born. Only then will they produce fewer. The mothers need the confidence that when they leave the clinical reassurance of the hospital, and take their babies home, death will not be lurking in the village waiting for their little ones.

Among both pastoral and cultivating cultures, the two minimal conditions of survival are *hygiene* and *clean water*. The first - hygiene - is a matter of knowledge and awareness. African mothers need to understand what is at stake when they cook near a lavatory, or when they feed a baby in a bottle that has not been sterilized. If African women are traditional custodians of fire and water for the home, they need to know how to mobilize fire in order to make water safe. The secret of boiling water as a method of disinfection is at hand.

Pastoralists are chronically short of clean water and even more lax in hygiene. Fertility is low among them as the lifestyle is significantly nomadic. Infant mortality among pastoralists is higher than among cultivators.

The Sociology of Water

Hygiene is sometimes part of a wider culture - and could even be linked to religion. Muslim Africa (both pastoral and agricultural) has a complicated relationship with the concept of 'clean water'. What defines clean is not necessarily 'fit to drink', but 'fit for ablution'. The devout Muslim prays five times a day - and each prayer is usually preceded by the use of water for ablution. This involves wetting hands, arms, feet, head and having a mouthwash before every prayer. At least traditionally, water is 'clean' when it is suitable for such preparation for worship. Clearly the standards of water suitable for sacred purposes are not the same as the standards suitable for human consumption. In the modern age many Muslim families have indeed recognized a dual standard of cleanliness - but in the rural areas in much of Muslim Africa there is a belief that if water is good enough for communication with God, it is good enough for consumption by human beings. Water for ablution does not have to be boiled. It simply requires careful assessment as to whether it has been *ritually* polluted. Bird droppings falling in the water can be ritual pollution - but the diseased hand of a believer is not. In terms of human dignity this scale of values is correct. However, in terms of human health more generally, it is not necessarily so.

Then there is the Muslim use of water after personal excretion. Islam does not encourage the use of toilet paper; it normally prescribes the use of water itself. Muslims believe that toilet paper does not clean everything from the relevant organ of the body after excretion. Only a thorough wash of that part of the body can restore the believer's ritual cleanliness. This is very hygienic in principle - but it does require that the believer subsequently cleans the left hand thoroughly after it has cleaned the anus. Normally this works all right, especially since orthodox Islam discourages believers from having long fingernails. Residual excreta in the nails of the left hand are normally cleared away with additional washing and soap (if soap can be afforded). However, when water generally is in short supply, these standards of thoroughness may become more lax. The risk of spreading infection from one believer to another could suddenly rise. The fingernails of the left hand could suddenly become major carriers of contagion. Indeed, death could lurk in the fingernails.

Perhaps the most hygienic use of water prescribed by Islam concerns sex. Between copulation and the believer's next prayer, a thorough wash of the body (a thorough shower) is needed. Every inch of the body needs to be washed - including the hair. Those who need to have sex every night are therefore enjoined to have a thorough shower every night - *after* sex. By the time of the dawn prayer the next morning the believer should have got rid of *janaba*, the unholy condition of sexual hedonism. Only a thorough shower can get rid of *janaba*. It is a major sin to enter a mosque before one has had his or her post-sex shower.

It is one of the ironies of history that a religion born in the grandeur of the Arabian Desert, in all its barrenness, should have prescribed so many ritual uses of water. Christianity seems to have the concept of a once-for-all baptism for each individual. In Islam, baptism is in a sense a daily affair - covering five prayers and following every sexual act. When available, water in Islam is a continual ritual necessity. In itself, all this is a contribution to hygiene. The problem arises when water is in short supply - and short cuts are made to make the same amount of water serve too many purposes. A little pond near the village may be used by too many believers to get rid of the post-sex *janaba* - 'the morning after the night before'. If one of the believers is diseased, the danger of infection arises. Islam is indeed a religion of cleanliness. Islam also recognizes that ritual cleanliness is no substitute for real hygienic consciousness.

Even an understanding of hygiene is not enough, if it is not accompanied by actual availability of clean water. Contaminated water is a killer. They say that in much of Africa it is easier to get a bottle of good beer than a glass of clean water. Things are not made easier when - as we indicated - western companies dump powdered milk on Africa that is then mixed with unclean water. Rural mothers are being diverted from the healthier tradition of breast-feeding. Africa needs birth control far less than it needs *death control*. We need family planning far less than family survival.

Yet in spite of all this death and devastation, Africa is the fastest growing continent in the world in terms of population. Droughts come and go, famine hits and retreats, disease is ever present in our midst, civil disorder takes its toll - and yet a new and larger generation of Africans is in the making all the time. The population of pastoralists may be shrinking, but the population of cultivators is larger than ever.

I am a citizen of Kenya, a country that seems to lead the world in population growth. I am a native of a continent that is in the vanguard of human fertility. Yet the world is staging spectacular singing and sporting events to save us from starvation and death. Why is the land of fertility also the land of famine? Why are a people of fecundity endowed with a continent of barrenness? It does not seem to be fair. It does not even make sense.

Yet all is not lost if Africans are capable of such astonishing growth-rates - if we can replace our dead so convincingly. Perhaps part of the explanation lies in the continuing resilience of the African family, in the mutual support it fosters among its members, and in that incredible love for children that is the hallmark of our remarkable continent. After all, the first human child ever was born there - a couple of million years ago. Yes, Africa invented the family. The family tradition continues, among both lovers of land and lovers of animals in Africa.

> The stream of experience meanders on
> In the vast expanse of the valley of time
> The new is come and the old is gone
> The land abides a changing clime.

Notes

[1] I am indebted to the late Okot p'Bitek, the Ugandan anthropologist and poet, for stimulation and information about myths of womanhood in northern Uganda. Okot and I also discussed similarities and differences between African concepts of matter and the ideas of Empedocles, the Greek philosopher of the fifth century BC.

References

BBC/WETA (1985-6) television project, 'The Africans: A Triple Heritage'.

Cutrufelli, M. R. (1983), *Women of Africa: Roots of Oppression,* London, Zed Press.

Hay, M. J. (1976), 'Luo Women and Economic Change During the Colonial Period', in N. J. Hafkin and E. G. Bay (eds) *Women in Africa: Studies in Social and Economic Change,* Stanford, California: Stanford University Press.

Mazrui, A. (1986), *The Africans: A Triple Heritage,* London: BBC Publications; New York: Little Brown.

P'Bitek, O. (1971), *African Religions in Western Scholarship,* Nairobi: East African Literature Bureau.

5 Breaking the Vicious Circle: Refugees and Other Displaced Persons in Africa

B. E. Harrell-Bond

> The presence of floating groups of oppressed and miserable persons presents the international community today with one of its greatest challenges.
>
> (Lillich, 1984, p. 63)

This discussion of refugees and other displaced persons in Africa[1] is taking place at a time when opinion in much of the world is hardening against refugees and when some European countries are openly violating the 1951 UN Conventions by *refouling* or repatriating refugees against their will. Refugees are being increasingly portrayed as a world-wide social problem of growing magnitude.

It is not that there are presently more refugees than before. Post-World War II Europe and other industrialized regions of the world accommodated far greater numbers of refugees than any source claims exist today, but today's refugees do not typically share the culture and religion of the rich countries. Today the majority of forced migrants are Africans. As Cuny and Stein (1988) put it, 'A prominent feature of today's refugees is that there are not necessarily more refugees, rather that there are more without solutions or awaiting solutions.'

The once traditional option for 'solving' refugee crises - resettlement - is fast disappearing. Moreover, as experience over the past few years has demonstrated, restrictionism - even in Africa - has become a very contagious disease. Thus refugee challenges in Africa are of necessity going to be addressed in Africa, chiefly by Africans and their governments with international assistance.

Discussions of new approaches to assistance are often bogged down by a general sense of impotence to effect the necessary political changes that would relieve the massive suffering of those affected. It may be that this pessimistic view is unwarranted. Certainly it is not possible to consider new approaches to the problems of refugees and other displaed peoples without first examining the political interests that cause involuntary migration, that keep the community of states from taking effective preventative or curative actions, and that influence both the amounts of funding avialable and the current approaches to assisting these victims.

When we turn to the current situation of aid provision for refuges in Africa, as outlined below, we see that responses to refugees illustrate a number of critical weaknesses. Underlying the failures of current approaches is the failure to address the political issues that are involved: both in considering the causes of involuntary migrations and the responses to it.

After outlining the context of the current refugee situation in Africa, I would like to offer a few new perspectives. While the objective here is to formulate new approaches to the social and economic problems of Africa, it should be noted from the outset that new approaches that are practicable must be designed for particular communities in specific contexts and, as such, must necessarily be informed by in-depth field research, a subject that will be discussed below.

In 1984 the Refugee Studies Programme at the University of Oxford[2] organized an international symposium entitled, 'Assistance to Refugees: Alternative Viewpoints'. It was attended by refugees, including eighteen who came directly from Africa, government officials, agency staff and academics. The recommendations and resolutions that were produced by this meeting still have great relevance and form an appendix to this chapter.

The Causes of African Refugee Flight and Responses to it

An International Dynamic

There is an urgent need for African governments to join with the donor and potential resettlement governments to re-think their attitudes concerning refugees and displaced peoples in Africa in order to find new approaches that will allow refugees to contribute their energies to genuine pro-ductive development. It is well known that the development of the agricultural economies of countries such as the USA, Canada, Australia, Brazil and France depended highly on the skills and energies of immigrants, many of whom were refugees in actuality if not in name. Even though the same conditions that existed in these countries may not obtain today in Africa, given Africa's tolerance for heterogeneity, perhaps forced upon it by the diversity of populations within any country, it should still be possible for African governments to take advantage of the skills of involuntary migrants and to begin to experiment with refugees' re-sourcefulness in new situations.

Even so, the prevalent attitude of both aid-givers and host governments towards the uprooted in Africa is that refugees are a burden and the only solution is their quick return to their country of origin. Voluntary repatriation has become a priority for donor and concerned governments for reasons other than the time being opportune or the condi-tions being conducive for repatriation. Enthusiasm for repa-triation appeals to the donors because it is cheaper and it is easier for the High Commissioner to justify to donors his office's humanitarian intervention in such programmes than in continuing to provide support for communities of the chronically displaced. As a result, some governments have co-operated with the implementation of policies designed to encourage repatriation of refugees back to the very same situations that led to their exodus. Given current thinking about refugees, there is little prospect that any other African host is prepared to follow the precedent set by Tanzania when it granted citizenship to a large segment of its refugee population. Even if they were willing, in many countries the flows of refugees are of such magnitude as to rule out permanent integration. Even if African governments (and refugees) are unwilling to consider the possibility of full integration, a different approach to assistance could permit refugees to contribute to the host's economy during their stay while at the same time ensuring that the funds attracted from international sources make a lasting developmental impact in the areas that are affected.

A major assumption underlies this discussion. This is that the capacity of African economies to absorb refugee populations can be strengthened by adopting the recommendations of the July 1984 international meeting of the Second International Conference on Assistance to Refugees in Africa. These called for incorporating planning for refugee communities into the regional planning of the host government and applying the lessons learned in the field of development. To do this, it will be necessary to educate the donors about the problems caused by earmarking aid solely for refugees. At least two major pieces of research, one exclusively focused on unassisted, spontaneously settled refugees (Harrell-Bond, 1986; Kuhlman, 1987) have shown that where assistance programmes are directed towards resolving the economic and social deprivations that result from dramatic demographic changes without distinguishing recipients, then economic, and perhaps even some social 'integration' (and thus the protection of the refugees) are better achieved. Where programmes are pinpointed to refugees, the perception of refugees under the aid 'umbrella' as privileged leads to resentment and an escalation of tensions between them and their hosts. If both gain hostilities are reduced. Moreover, such an approach would ensure from the outset that aid budgets would have a lasting impact on the host's economy. As it is they disappear into the 'black hole' of relief.

What is being emphasised here is that considering the enormous economic problems of African countries, the issue of making the host country a tolerable and liveable sanctuary for refugees is just as important as offering asylum (Karadawi, 1983).

It is necessary to recognize the connection between political and economic arrangements of a state (including the host state) and to identify underlying national causes of uprootedness - the failure of states to provide for the basic human rights of its citizens (physical security, vital subsistence, and liberty of political participation and physical movement). In many cases states could make significant progress in providing their citizenry with these basic needs even without greater resources than already available. Where there is a genuine resource scarcity, then international assistance should be concentrated on their provision.

Present approaches to assistance have been organized on the assumption that the problems of refugees are short term. These approaches have been shown to be wasteful of the resources that refugees bring to their host community, to exacerbate tensions between them and their hosts, and to encourage dependency. Moreover, the failure to insist that international assistance be used to build up the material and institutional capacity of host countries has resulted in a greater dependency than ever before on the efforts of foreign non-governmental agencies (NGOs) to administer externally funded assistance. Today in this regard many African states are much less self-reliant than ever before. As one writer put it:

'Ad-hockism' dominates refugee programmes. Last-minute airlifts of food parcels and blankets to stricken refugee communities continue to remain the 'bread and butter' of refugee work. Apart from a few instances here and there, the international community has not moved one inch towards a 'developmental' approach to alleviating the problems of refugees, and making them more self-reliant and self-respecting. The 'hand-outs' approach continues to remain the dominant approach. (Tandon, 1988)

This ad hoc approach is, of course, highly political. It has deep implications for relations between refugees and aid givers, and between the latter and relevant governments. Consider the image of 'the refugee'. Although one UNHCR poster continues to remind the public that *Einstein was a refugee*, the great majority of contemporary media and agency images give the impression that refugees are undifferentiated 'masses' or 'flows', and no longer comprise groups of individuals with personal histories, skills, and aspirations, with varying capacities for strategic planning and decision-making, and with different human needs or feelings such as hope, joy, despair and pain. Most assistance for refugees in Africa is organized on the premise that the recipients are illiterate peasant farmers who do not know what they want or need or how to achieve it. As a result (and despite Africa's widespread need for technically trained personnel), the enormous investments that have been made in the education and training of thousands of Africans who have subsequently become refugees is being wasted. More generally, paternalistic aid provision continues, based on the assumption that refugees are incapable of making critical decisions about their own lives.

Elsewhere (Harrell-Bond, 1986, p. 26) I have discussed the problem of the false premises upon which much humanitarian assistance is based and noted how western notions of compassion tend to be ethnocentric and paternalistic; 'It is the moral loading of humanitarian assistance which denies the need for review and prevents scrutiny.' There is a need for researchers to examine and document not only how lack of deep knowledge of other societies, but also how differences in language, class, culture and negative stereotypes, influence policies and practices concerning refugees today.

Forces Creating Refugees

Any conceptualization of the refugee problem that limits the responsibilities of industrialized nations merely to a humanitarian role, ignores their part in the problems that cause refugee flows. Refugees in the Horn or Southern Africa, for example are not simply the result of localized conflict. Refugees are a symptom of power struggles within the world system, and the economic, strategic and other interests of industrialized states must be incorporated into the study of the factors that give rise to the refugee phenomenon today.

Though there have been calls for 'political will' (Hocke, 1986) to resolve the refugee problem, 'political will' like 'humanitarianism' can be part of the semantics of a mystification of the reality. The community of states (both worldwide and in Africa) has not yet produced a 'leviathan' to effectively arbitrate between conflicting interests that, if unresolved, may create refugee flows (Karadawi, 1983). And so there is much evidence that the political will that creates refugees is, to date, more powerful than the political will to resolve the situations that generate them. An approach that could pre-empt or prevent refugee flows needs to be developed in a context that particularly gives opportunity for refugees to articulate their own views. For example, how to make repatriation an act of will, rather than the result of negotiations that have been conducted over their heads by the UNHCR and government authorities.

Some would argue that until the structural defects of the world states system have been corrected, African states will continue to be overwhelmed by refugees. There is no sign of the world system being changed in the near future, rather we see more and more evidence in Africa of an escalation of the retrogressive process, the seeds of which were sown centuries ago.

Wherever in the world there have been wars, revolutions, or the breakdown of the distribution system, there have been massive movements of people. Since independence, Africa has known its full share of all three, chiefly because of disputes over control of central power, its lack of control over its own economic resources and unsolved questions of boundaries. This has also made African countries highly vulnerable to the consequences of power struggles between the west and the east, and the drive of industrialized countries to find markets for their goods, including armaments, equipment, and expertise to be used in massive development projects. Few of these latter have been successful, though they have left enormous debts that have made African governments still more liable to challenge by their own people. Moreover, the requirements of many development projects have themselves caused massive displacement. In some cases the construction of dams, roads and railways, involving compulsory relocation, have been undertaken in the national interest. In too many cases, however, development projects only benefit a minority of the population and peasants have been rendered landless in the drive to expand cash crops to service debts where the borrowed capital was not invested to increase productivity.

The same forces that generate refugees also work towards a loss of sovereignty in the countries of asylum and in the countries from which refugees flee. The numbers are often such that they represent a burden beyond the means of any country to absorb on its own. This inevitably leads to the activity of a host of multinational and non-governmental agencies. In some regions of Africa these are now so locally prominent as to take over large areas of governance. Inevitably the independence with which they act and the special relationship they create with refugees has an impact on the local citizenry, who compare the well-financed operations of the agencies with the poverty of their own governments. At the same time the existence of displaced people in the country of origin encourages NGOs to claim the right (always in the name of humanitarian values), to operate independently in provisioning them and otherwise providing basic necessities. The reputation of the home government thereby suffers, and it loses international credibility as a responsible government able to maintain security for life and livelihood. The very presence of such powerful aid providers may even hinder the development of government infrastructure.

Referring to Africa as a continent poised on the brink of destruction, Zia Rizvi traces the vicious circle of the conjoining crises that have led to the uprooting of millions of people.

> The way things now stand, it is no more a question of hypotheses of catastrophe in a few years: the catastrophe is already there. . .massive displacements of population are going to shake up the social fabric which is already weak, the economic structure which is also weak, the political structure which is. . .fragile. That is going to lead to violence, and violence is going to lead to repression and repression is going to lead to bad planning and poverty. . .and that is going to lead to displacement and so on. The vicious circle will be complete in Africa; perhaps it already is, and we are just closing our eyes. (1984)

How then can African states prevent or at the very least reduce the size and incidence of mass exoduses? How, given the economic crises that face most host governments, can they meet the needs of refugees within their borders?

Few governments have been able to meet the expectations of their populations for development of the sort that had been so long denied them by their colonial overlords. More to the point concerning the creation of refugees, even the scarce resources available to African states have only benefited certain regions or groups within their societies. The resulting inadequacies in technology, infrastructure, and unequal methods of distribution within countries have left large sections of the population without the basis for sustaining even a minimal level of subsistence. These disparities have become one basis for internal challenges to state authority. As Shacknove has pointed out:

> In exhange for their allegiance, citizens can minimally expect that their government will guarantee physical security, vital subsistence, and liberty of political participation and physical movement. No reasonable person would be satisfied with less. Beneath this threshold the social compact has no meaning. . . .Moreover, because all of these needs are equally essential for survival, the violation of each constitutes an equally valid claim to refugeehood. (1985)

Few leaders have taken seriously the fact that the first responsibility of the state is to maintain a 'minimal social bond' between itself and its citizenry. As Shacknove has pointed out, a 'minimal bond of trust, loyalty, protection, and assistance has always existed between virtually every human being and some larger collectively - be it clan, feudal manor, or modern state'. The refugee is created when 'these minimal bonds are ruptured'.

> To the extent that a life-threatening situation occurs because of human actions rather than natural causes, the state has left unfulfilled its basic duty to protect the citizen from the actions of others. All other human rights are meaningless when starvation results from the neglect or malice of the local regime. Thus, in some dire circumstances, what appears on the surface to be the result of natural forces may, on closer scrutiny, reveal state negligence or indifference. As with threats to physical security, when the state is unwilling or unable to protect a citizen from the life-threatening actions of others, the basis for a legitimate claim to refugeehood is generated. (Ibid.)

As Shacknove reminds us, 'Threats to vital subsistence are subject to the same logic. To the extent that such threats to the survival of the citizen are due to human actions, they, like security threats and supposed "natural" calamities, create legitimate claims for state protection.' Except where there is a 'genuine resource scarcity', the citizen has a legitimate claim on the state for minimal subsistence.

There are other necessary conditions for the fulfilment of subsistence needs. These include: a technology for processing resources; an infrastructure for facilitating commerce, and a method of distribution. Shacknove reminds us that providing these only require a change in priorities since:

> None necessarily requires extensive capital investment, specialized knowledge, heroic governmental efforts, or saintly sacrifices by the local affluent in order to sustain a minimal level of subsistence. A hoe may be an altogether satisfactory tool for processing a resource and a footpath may suffice as a conduit for commerce. Similarly, a minimally satisfactory method of distribution (where no one suffers from a severe protein/caloric deficiency) is consistent with extensive inequalities of wealth. (1985)

The inability or failure of African states to provide for the basic human rights of their populations is compounded by the absence of solutions to (and the unwillingness to negotiate) the nationalities question, which continues to plague most independent African states and provoke power struggles. The ability of states to enforce the apparent stability previously enjoyed by colonial regimes through a state monopoly of violence is frustrated by international involvement; for instance in the easy transfer of arms to insurgents. However, the monopoly of force held by the colonizers should not be seen as positive; it contained in the short-term, and exacerbated in the long-term, the root causes of most refugee flows in Africa today.

The Numbers Game: 'Official' and 'Unofficial' Refugees

No one really knows how many refugees there are in Africa today. It has been estimated that at least one person in 200 is a refugee and the number is increasing daily. This estimated total, nearing six million, does not include the millions who have remained *inside* their national borders, displaced and often facing starvation. These refugees and displaced peoples are largely situated in the poorest countries of Africa. According to Kibreab (1988), of the 44 states, by 1986, 36 were somehow affected by refugees. Ten African states were both generating and hosting large numbers of refugees. Another 23 were providing asylum without themselves generating refugees and three were only refugee-producing. Kibreab notes how:

> In order to appeal for short and long-term assistance, both host governments and the UNHCR find it necessary to convert refugees into statistics and as a result figures based on 'educated guesses' are generated....Refugee statistics are by their very nature highly controversial and are rarely neutral. Host governments are often accused by the international donor agencies of deliberately exaggerating the numbers of refugees in their territories in order to maximize external assistance and the former accuse the latter of deliberate underestimation in order to minimize costs for themselves. (1988)

New approaches to assisting the uprooted must move beyond the numbers game. What has been forgotten in the arguments between governments and UNHCR is that the vast majority of refugees today are not living in refugee camps and are not recipients of international assistance. Stein and Clark (1984) estimated that at most 40 per cent of Africa's refugees were assisted. The most recent estimates put the figure of those who are the objects of aid at only 25 per cent! (Kibreab, 1988). As Karadawi (1983) has noted, the fact that these 'spontaneously settled' refugees are deprived of aid has been justified by the ethnocentric (even racist) argument of 'African hospitality' and ethnic lines across the borders. 'Even if this were true, it became a tragic paradox of African society - nurtured as Africans are with the idea that no individual should be sacrificed' (ibid.).

> The dubious nature of the argument of traditional hospitality cannot be overstressed. Communities in the host country do *not* always welcome the spontaneous settlement of refugees either because of traditional antagonism or fear of competition, or because of the effects of their own poverty, which can explain the Hobbesian state of nature. (Ibid.)

At times of a major influx, as Karadawi points out, 'The society as a whole often tends to collapse.' The idea of 'traditional' humanitarianism has been used as a convenient belief that 'absolves donor agencies and governments from identifying and helping to solve the problems that are so potentially great (ibid.). Moreover, it is often based on unproven assumptions about the ability of the hosts and the hosts' ecologies to support the establishment of these newcomers without deep personal sacrifices or ecological degradation.

Labelling the Refugee

Although the integration of refugees into the host society is said to be a major goal of international humanitarian agencies, the effect of categorizing men, women, and children who move across borders en masse as refugees and isolating them in camps actually impedes that process. Migration - both voluntary and involuntary - is not a new phenomenon in Africa. From the dawn of history, African people have received strangers and have established customs and rituals for incorporating them into their communities. The idea of large numbers of people, labelled refugees, who have not been incorporated into the host society in Africa is relatively new. In fact, it is argued that the international system of states is in itself a major factor in creating categories of persons, making, labelling and perpetuating refugees as a problem in Africa and elsewhere. Those who have been captured by the state-sponsored assistance programmes have been frozen in a permanent state of marginality in their host societies.

People often argue that refugees are (at least categorically) the inevitable result of the rise of nation-states and national boundaries. However, mass movements have occurred even in recent times in which the victims were not labelled as refugees by the receiving country. For example, during the regime of Sekou Touré, tens of thousands of Fula-speaking people fled Guinea. Even though the Guinea Government had *extremely* close relationships at the time with the government of Sierra Leone, the Fula were, for the most part, peacefully received by Sierra Leone, perhaps because the country had sufficient resources to be able to share (Harrell-Bond et al., 1977). No international assistance programmes were mounted; no camps were set up. The Sierra Leone Government permitted the integration of the Fula into the national economy to which, no doubt, research could demonstrate that they have since made a valuable contribution. Some Fula were employed in urban centres as unskilled labourers. Many involved themselves in trade (including diamonds). Most were cattle-keepers. Their leadership was absorbed into the Islamic religious community, where they were held in very high esteem. One was even elected as the 'headman' of all the Fula in the capital city, Freetown.

Although there were incidents of conflict between local farmers and the Fula cattle-herders over land use, these were settled in the mosques or in the local courts that administered customary law in the same manner as in any other dispute. Generally speaking, probably no greater conflict occurred between the Fula and local people than had existed within the local community before they arrived. Oddly enough, one might argue that one of the main advantages the Fula had over typical 'camp refugees' was that the Sierra Leone Government did not receive assistance from the United Nations High Commissioner and international non-governmental agencies. If they had, it would have been necessary to impose the category 'refugee' upon those who would be beneficiaries of outside aid. It would also have been seen necessary to isolate these 'refugees' in order that aid would not 'leak out' to those who were not refugees. Fula were incorporated into the host society and did not become dependent on an assistance programme. Present approaches to assistance have the paradoxical effect of cutting refugees off from the possibilities of making such an adaptation. It is not surprising that, running right through agency literature, there is the common theme describing refugees as suffering from the 'dependency syndrome' (Waldron, 1987; Zetter, 1987). Is this not a classic case of blaming the victim?

Why then are camps so often a preferred solution? Many African governments eye refugees with suspicion because refugees are seen to be committed to changing the government that led to their expulsion. Despite the fact that only a very small proportion of any refugee community is 'political' in this way, such suspicion has often been the excuse for confining refugees to camps and for the authoritarian administrative systems that exist in many camps and settlements. The major reason refugees are put in organized settlements is to facilitate the distribution of material assistance that has been earmarked for them by the international community. As others have observed, the aid community prefers to 'work with passive, non-politicised refugees' (Karadawi et al., 1987). One might go further and ask why it is that agencies concentrate so definitively on the provision of aid to such 'captured' refugees rather than on the conditions that generated refugees in the first place. Why is it that:

The generally-accepted role of the agencies has been to solve refugees' problems in the host country. Aid has therefore been confined to the *symptoms* of the problem. The basic constraint of assistance is intrinsic to the idea of it. Assistance to cure the symptom would incarcerate the refugee phenomenon as a threat to the status quo. Whereas the international community has proved incapable of restoring human rights against persecution by the state, the alternative it has pursued has been first to avoid the identity of each persecuted group and try to create the uniformity of a new person called 'refugee' - who should be reinstated within the state system. It has aimed to finish the marginal legal status by creating a sociological tribe of pariahs. The political sentiments of each refugee group are to be suppressed - even by the host country. (Karadawi, 1983)

It is also argued by some that camp conditions both deter others from seeking asylum and encourage those who fled to return home. There is no reason to think that those who have chosen to settle themselves have lost the ability to decide to return if and when conditions improve at home.

Instead of impeding repatriation, a fear some may express, approaches to assistance that permit refugees to be incorporated into the host economy may actually enhance the possibilites of refugees successfully returning to their home country when conditions are conducive. The largest number of repatriating Ugandans appear to have been those who were spontaneously settled in the Sudan. Reports from Sierra Leone suggest that since the death of Sekou Touré most Fula have returned to Guinea.

The Promulgation of the 1969 OAU Convention

The first occasion for African refugees to come to international attention was during the Algerian war for independence. Subsequent anti-colonial wars in Africa created large numbers of refugees, but the vast majority were accommodated in neighbouring countries that sympathized with these struggles against a common enemy. Thus, during the early post-colonial period, African states viewed refugees as temporary, a 'problem' that would disappear once Africa was rid of European domination. It was in this political context that the 1969 Organization of African Unity (OAU) Convention Governing the Specific Aspects of Refugee Problems in Africa was promulgated.

At the time of the founding of the OAU, pan-Africanism was an ideal espoused by some prominent African leaders. It stressed that ultimately there should be one united African state, rather than a continent artificially divided by the state boundaries of the colonizers. The ideal was rendered impracticable as the government elites sought to preserve their independent authority and status. However, the establishment of the OAU aimed to provide a mechanism for some unity of action with the emphasis upon finding African solutions for African problems.

The OAU Convention expanded on the definition of a refugee as laid down by the United Nations in 1951 (which it adopted) by including, in addition to individual persecution, those who seek asylum as a result of external aggression, occupation, foreign domination or events seriously disturbing public order. It permitted the practice of accepting refugees en masse on *prima facie* evidence. Thus the OAU definition recognized that 'The normal bond between the citizen and the state can be severed in diverse ways, persecution being but one.' It also recognized that, 'Societies periodically disintegrate because of their frailty rather than because of their ferocity, victims of domestic division or foreign intervention' (Shacknove, 1985).

The OAU Convention, unlike the 1951 UN Convention, assumed that refugees would want to return home. It makes explicit reference to repatriation. The need to confirm its volutary character is emphasized and the provision is included that every possible assistance should be given by governments, voluntary agencies, international and inter-governmental organizations to facilitate the refugees' safe return.

The office of the United Nations High Commissioner for Refugees (UNHCR), had been campaigning to stretch the definition beyond the confines of the 1951 Convention since 1956. It advised and participated in the drafting of the OAU Convention, which it regarded as an achievement and a model that should be applied outside the region. Given the example set by the OAU and the success of the combined efforts of Africans and their European advisers to expand the definition of a refugee to accord with the kinds of situations that were recreating involuntary migrations, it is disappointing to find a growing cynicism, especially among humanitarians in Europe, concerning the motivations of asylum seekers from the so-called Third World. One can observe a noticeable shift away from concern with the welfare of the individual to the emphasis upon 'mass exodus'. Moreover, we are told by international agencies that refugees can be manipulated by the 'pull' factor of aid and suffer the 'dependency syndrome'. Most dangerous of all in terms of promoting further negative attitudes towards refugees, we are told that many are not refugees at all, but economic migrants, opportunists, even 'fortune seekers' simply looking for a better life (Waldron, 1987; Hocke, 1986).

The OAU Convention and Interstate Relations

While the OAU Convention defined the granting of asylum to refugees as a peaceful and humanitarian act, it was written against the background of the formation of newly independent states that were seeking to establish legitimacy and consolidate internal control. This influenced its content. The cornerstone upon which the Organization of African Unity had been built was the sanctity of borders existing on the attainment of independence as well as on the principles of 'territorial integrity' and 'non-interference in the internal affairs of member states'. Just prior to the founding of the OAU, Eritrea had been annexed by Ethiopia and already refugees had reached the Sudan as a result of the Eritrean war for independence. Other refugee-producing conflicts such as the civil war in Sudan and uprisings in what is now Zaire also influenced thinking about the administration of refugee populations by host governments.

Thus, while the OAU definition of a refugee may be seen to be more liberal than the UN Convention, the caveats that were included could be used to undermine its stated purpose: the protection of refugees. The effect of these caveats was to place an overriding priority on the protection of the rights and interests of states. First, and perhaps most dangerous of all if it were implemented, the Convention gives the host state the power to determine when those circumstances in the country of origin that caused it to give refugee status have ceased to exist. It permits states to deny refugee status to any person who has been 'guilty of acts contrary to the purposes and principles of the OAU or the UN'. In the interests of interstate relations, it requires that refugees be settled away from the frontier of their country of origin.

Signatories to the Convention undertake the responsibility to ensure that refugees are prohibited from attacking any member of the OAU 'through subversive activities, especially through arms, press, and radio, which may cause tension between Member States'. Thus, if states strictly observed the Convention, refugees would only be tolerated if politically passive. Consequently, despite the fact that refugees, by their very nature, desire political change in their home state so that they can return, states have agreed to support each other in the prevention of activity to promote change. Thus, if a host state were to follow the Convention to the letter, refugee status would certainly not be accorded to 'freedom fighters' who are seeking to overthrow the government of another member state.

In reality refugees are characterized by their home government as the enemy across the border. The general attitude has been whoever gives asylum to an enemy is himself an enemy, and African states have largely failed to avoid interstate tensions over refugee issues. In many cases refugees have actually been used as the pawns in interstate relations. The priority given to interstate relations over the needs of the communities that have been uprooted has justified many African states in viewing refugees as a security risk and imposing on them a militaristic administrative structure. It has also given support to the policy of placing refugees in camps rather than permitting them the basic human right of freedom of movement. Freedom of movement is essential if they are to use their skills and energies in productive ways that will also contribute to the host economy. Moreover, the 'sacred' principle of non-interference in the internal affairs of member states has been used as a justification for the failure of members of the OAU to take any action against states that produce refugees.

The Politics of Assistance to Refugees

> Why is it that every US dollar comes with twenty Americans attatched to it? (Alternative Viewpoints, 1984)

> We must re-orient ourselves to the reality of the [present] situation. . . International organizations were established. . .to serve certain categories and groups and communities. They should be. . .re-oriented to serve the new situation. . .[which is] multi-racial, multi-cultural. . .I think people of the African countries should. . .share in decision-making. . .on the operational side. . . .Monies should be used more effectively. Not on salaries, air-fares, not on extending the image of an alien administration and alien ways of doing things, but on an indigenous, effective way of handling a situation . . .The refugee needs to be involved. . .[she or] he should be handled as a dignified human being. (Alternative Viewpoints, 1984)

So long as the interests of states remain paramount to the needs of the uprooted in Africa, it is necessary to address the question of the politics of assistance before talking about new approaches to their problems. People may 'feel' humanitarian towards others in dire need, but only ostriches can ignore the fact that every action has some political consequences.

Appeals for refugee assistance after World War II (when most of the uprooted orginated in Eastern Europe), were overtly political, but when the office of the UN High Commissioner for Refugees was established, its work was defined as being entirely non-political. Be this as it may, in an emergency, the availability of external assistance to African states is always conditioned by the political interests of the *primarily* western donors and their clients, the intergovernmental and non-governmental aid agencies. For example Sudan's ability to attract sufficient external funding to assist the several refugee nationalities within its borders has always been affected by the attitudes of western governments towards the Sudanese Government, its relationship with the governments of the countries of origin and, most recently, by the west's warming relations with its neighbour, Ethiopia.

This is not to say that cold political calculation is the only motive for giving aid. There is considerable humanitarian concern behind the assistance given by many external donors, which aim to make resources available that will alleviate suffering and promote more democratic forms of government. They face a dilemma, however, when seeking to act on these moral precepts. To establish a presence in a country in order to give assistance to the needy may lend unwished-for credibility to oppressive governments. Conversely, supplying aid through liberation movements implies political commitment to efforts to ovethrow recognized regimes - and often commitment to particular ideological positions. The dilemma is not so great for those donors and agencies that support the work of the African National Congress (ANC) or the South West African Peoples' Organization (SWAPO), because of UN and OAU upport for these two organizations and because of general international

condemnation of apartheid. But even here there are dilemmas. What about those refugees who do not actively support
such organizations? Most other situations are far less clear-
cut. As for example, when there are uprooted people on both
sides of a border. In war situations it is often the case that
there are more displaced or starving people within the
contested region than there are people who have managed
to cross a border and are accessible to assistance.

Should international assistance for uprooted and displaced peoples only be directed through recognized states?
Estimates put the numbers of uprooted southern Sudanese
huddled around Khartoum and the major cities of eastern
Sudan at 3 million, with another 300,000 or so living as
refugees in Ethiopia. In theory (although not likely in practice), none of these people should be malnourished or starving, since they are fully accessible to the governments and
international aid agencies. What about the millions trapped
in the war-torn south? Through international NGOs, some
governments, of course, are providing support to these
people, but one of the effects certainly is to internationalize
the conflict. Perhaps such external support even serves to
prolong it.

Yet not to provide aid is also deeply political. Twice in
this decade thousands of drought-victims from Eritrea and
Tigray have been forced to cross the Sudan border because
governments were unwilling to allow (or provide) sufficient
supplies to reach the areas where they lived because of wars
that no one could win. Even when they reached the Sudan,
unknown numbers met their death through starvation because of shortages of food and shelter, shortages that were
mainly the result of debates over whose responsibility they
were, and whether they were *real* refugees (i.e., of concern to
the office of the UNHCR). When the rains came again, with
financial assistance from some international NGOs, the
Eritrea Relief Association and the Relief Society of Tigray
organized - at great expense in both lives and material
assistance - the repatriation of the civilians back into the

contested regions. This year, once again, with both locusts and a shortage of rainfall adversely affecting agriculture, thousands of people are at risk of starvation and are once more on the move.

The rich nations are neither morally bankrupt nor necessarily unwilling to allocate material aid despite the political implications. Some bilateral as well as some multi-lateral donors overtly use aid to re-establish direct control or to demand certain concessions from recipient governments. The Lomé Convention, for example is outspoken on the relevance of human rights issues. Today most sources for multilateral aid (donor governments, etc.) prefer to see their funds being used to bridge the gap between humanitarian relief aid and development aid, which is directed towards the general needs of areas affected by population move-ments be they refugees, nationals or returnees. Approaches that additionally required assistance to be invested in help-ing states uphold the human rights of their citizens, to satisfy their basic needs, could prevent further mass exoduses.

However, despite the impersonal, supposedly 'non-political' character of UNHCR, it may not continue to be viewed by donors or hosts as the best avenue for politically potent refugee assistance. In this new climate, could local NGOs be seen to offer a better alternative for the donors?

Considering present-day realities, UNHCR may even-tually have to redefine its role and its priorities. Even with less finance, the office of the UNHCR still has an important role to play, but it will have to adapt its organization. A UNHCR that is not taking the leading role in refugee assis-tance means a UNHCR that must place protection in the forefront of its work. It will have more time to become, once again, the platform for the powerless refugees, the role for which it was intended. However, to play this role, it must re-define protection in the light of the realities of today's refugee situation, and must find more effective ways of upholding their human rights. Some would argue that assistance is the 'other side of the coin' of protection, but as has been demonstrated, aid that is earmarked for refugees, excluding their (sometimes even poorer) hosts *creates* security problems for refugees (Harrell-Bond, 1986, chapter 4).

The 'Politics' of Aid Administration

Host countries are alarmingly dependent upon aid agencies. Yet there is rarely an opportunity for indigenous professionals to question the agencies' approach or contribute to the general theoretical debate concerning their role in assistance. It would sometimes appear that host governments, like refugees, are expected to receive assistance without questioning either the suitability of the gift or the competence of the giver. (Karadawi, 1983)

The international development community, in some respects, is an Alice-in-Wonderland world with a logic of its own, bewildering to one who first encounters it expecting it to be primarily oriented to improving the lot of the peoples of developing nations. Goals enunciated on high clash with one another, and with practice on the ground. Other apparent absurdities include the provision of technical advice which is patently inappropriate in the context within which it is to be implemented, the clinging to tried routines which have failed in the past and are likely to fail again, the commissioning of and payment for reports destined only to be filed, the endless succession of workshops and conferences which consume energies and budgets, and the way in which information is bracketed out. (Colson, 1982)

The office of the UN High Commissioner for Refugees was established in 1951 with an international mandate to protect the human rights of refugees. In seeking to protect refugees, UNHCR limits itself to persuasion through secret diplomacy. As an intergovernmental organization that must raise funds for each new refugee emergency, UNHCR is relatively powerless *vis-à-vis* the small 'club' of governments that support its budget. It therefore lacks sufficient independence to use publicity as a method of sanctioning govern-

ments that contravene the international refugee conventions
or basic human rights. This was demonstrated recently by
the High Commissioner's decision to destroy the January
1988 issue of *Refugees* that carried what has been described
by other UNHCR staff as some very mild criticism of the
German government's treatment of refugees (Woodford,
1988).

Vis-à-vis governments that host refugees, UNHCR can
only provide its services with permission, and such permission may not be forthcoming, particularly in cases where
states are not parties to the conventions. Its chief leverage
here is the potential humanitarian aid that would flow as a
result of granting permission. Once established in a country,
it clearly can use its power over funds to influence the host
government's assistance policy.

In at least one case in Africa a state actually rejected aid
that UNHCR proferred and, like Sierra Leone, managed to
cope with an influx of refugees without relying on assistance
from outside its borders. During the war against the Portuguese in Guinea-Bissau, refugees fled both to Senegal and
Guinea. UNHCR established an office and administered
assistance in Senegal. Sekou Touré neither invited UNHCR
to establish an office in Conakry, nor accepted its offers of
assistance for the refugees. Even though there was no evidence at all that refugees were either unprotected by the host
state or needed more material than the Guinea people could
provide, the then High Commissioner undertook a special
mission to Conakry to try to persuade Sekou Touré to
reverse his decision (Jaeger, 1988). This displays a general
characteristic of all bureaucracies, to cultivate opportunities
for widening their sphere of activity, to evoke their manifest
charter to enhance their prestige, and to serve their own
interests as an expanding organization even when that
function is already being provided by others.

Even when it had become clear that the place of action
would be outside Europe in Asia and Africa, it was necessary
for UNHCR to overcome reluctance within UN circles to

allow this office to extend its activities beyond the function of protection and to become involved in implementing assistance programmes for refugees. Today, however, UNHCR is the conduit for most international funds for assisting refugees. Assistance programmes are the main focus of its work in Africa. Its staff and budget have dramatically expanded over the past decade. Since 1982 this office has been expanding its role in also chanelling assistance to 'returnees'. Following ICARA II, with its emphasis on assisting 'refugee-affected' areas, the EEC has made special funds available under Lomé III, Article 204 to support infrastructural development in such regions. UNHCR has also sought control over some of these funds for its programmes, which if carried out according to the guidelines of Article 204, would directly involve it in development projects for areas affected by involuntary migration, a role it is not so far equipped to undertake.

The Growing Power of International NGOs

The growing crisis of mass exodus since the late 1970s has spawned an ever-increasing number of international non-governmental organizations that are now deeply involved in refugee assistance. For the most part, UNHCR does not itself implement assistance programmes; this is done by its 'partner', the NGOs. Many NGOs rely heavily, if not entirely, on funds from UNHCR for their overseas operations. Others seek funds directly from donor governments, the EEC, large foundations, and mainline charities. Heavy reliance on such funding has led to enormous competition among NGOs for contracts. Unfortunately in some cases winning a contract may depend more on an agency's home government's influence on UNHCR or other funding agency than on the NGO's competence to do the work in the field, for example, see Waldron (1984). Thus, it is not surprising that indigenous NGOs - especially those that are not the clones of northern NGOs - (for example, local committees) are rarely directly involved in refugee assistance even when such assistance is provided over many years. Neither is the UNHCR often forthcoming when refugee-based humanitarian organizations ask for support.

In crisis situations such as large influxes of refugees there is an even greater tendency among donors to cede control over the administration of funds to external agencies rather than to host governments or indigenous non-governmental agencies. This approach has been rationalized on the grounds that African states lack the administrative capacity to cope with an acute disaster and that emergency programmes are particularly prone to African financial mismanagement. This is a euphemistic way of expressing the perception that all African governments are corrupt. The inability of governments to cope with major emergencies is attributed to corruption. This is despite what experience has so often demonstrated: that *no* governments are ever adequately prepared for emergency situations and *all* lack fully rationalized and comprehensive systems of accounting for funds derived from diverse sources spent under such conditions. The idea of setting up special permanent offices to deal with disasters is very recent. Most governments, both rich and poor together, rely on ad hoc arrangements.

The assumption of local corruption leads also to inordinate attention being given to the question of accountability for government spending. It should be noted that 'accountability' in aid administration is itself usually profoundly distorted. It does not primarily mean direct assessment of how well such acute aid provision actually works. Instead, it centres on what is far easier to measure (and far more likely to support the bureaucratic status quo): financial accountability. Accountability is thus reduced to bookkeeping. It is also worth noting that no reciprocal system of 'accountability' ensures that outsiders are themselves accountable to the refugees they purport to assist, for the impact of the programmes they design, be it to their own constituencies or to their host governments.

In theory, international (or indigenous) agencies involved in refugee programmes should work in close partnership with the local administration. An emergency that leads to the arrival of trained professionals with experience in managing the logistics of aid should be an opportunity for the host government to strengthen its capacity to manage its own programmes after the humanitarians leave. Instead, there is unfortunately, a very great tendency for outsiders to mistake the poverty of a country for incompetence, and to inappropriately assume the role of the host. The excuse given for bypassing local government bureaucracies is the need for the speedy delivery of relief. The apparent lack of efficient administrative services (often equated with small offices and run-down equipment) is viewed as a lacuna that humanitarian organizations must step forward to fill. Since they are the conduit for outside funding, many agencies would be surprised if their right to make policy regarding refugee matters were questioned as well. There is an implicit assumption that international experience is a sufficient credential to get on with the work, whatever the local nuances. This is one of the chief paternalistic ideologies of what might be called the 'ideology of acute aid provision': that the humanitarian needs of a given situation are so great, so pressing, that one cannot wait to build up local structures of delivery.

Ironically, few expatriate agency staff actually have previous management experience of the kind they find so lacking in host government structures. Almost all lack knowledge of local rules and regulations and of social customs. The notion that people who work with refugees could benefit from, indeed should be required to have specialized training has as yet gained little currency. Usually work is undertaken as if nothing might be learned from consultation or benefit from team work. In the Sudan, when the office of the Commissioner for Refugees did attempt to have a say - to mitigate competition between agencies, to redress the imbalance between wasteful duplication of services in some areas to the neglect of others, or to require some standards of competency of agency personnel - the office was accused by agency staff of being 'militaristic' (Karadawi, 1982).

The structure for administering assistance to the uprooted within a particular state has important implications. It may reinforce the dominant top-down approach, and exacerbate the process of 'institutional destruction' (see Morss, 1984) while permitting outside agencies to gain greater control over policies and practice. It may not enhance the capacity of local government institutions or refugee-based organizations.

Creating Special Government Offices to Deal with Refugees

Many African governments have of necessity established special offices to deal with refugees and displaced peoples. These offices are typically added to the normal government bureaucracy. This has the effect of predetermining that funds earmarked for relief and/or short-term projects lie outside national planning structures. It also creates another layer of bureaucracy that develops its own momentum and survival interests, a wild card in the bureaucratic structure. The interest in maintaining and expanding such bureaucracies is further encouraged when outside funding pays for more jobs, with higher salaries and other benefits than civil servants could possibly enjoy elsewhere in the country. One should not be surprised to hear that upon the signing of the Geneva Accord, 1,000 local employees of the Commission for Afghan Refugees in Pakistan reacted sharply to the threat of the repatriation of the refugees, petitioning the government to preserve their employment. Institutionalizing such bureaucracies for the administration of refugee assistance outside the normal structures of the government could, therefore, encourage the perpetuation of the status of 'refugee'.

With the increase in funds available for humanitarian relief there is likely to be a sharp reduction of corresponding funds for development in an affected country. In Ethiopia, for example, the government office of the Relief and Rehabilitation Commission is responsible for all relief programmes. It has institutionalized nearly all aspects of relief management to the extent that it has duplicated many of the functions of other ministries. When, as is becoming more the case, the bulk of overseas assistance coming into a country is earmarked for emergency relief for the uprooted, other ministries are starved of funds. In the Sudan, the office of the Commissioner for Refugees has similarly been expanded and the staff salaries are supplemented by funds from UNHCR.

There are other negative consequences that may follow the centralizing of refugee administration within one conventional ministry of the government. Uganda has been receiving refugees since 1959. Until recently, government responsibility for refugees was under a normal government ministry, that of Youth, Culture and Sports. The settlement of refugees from Rwanda (who came with large herds of cattle) now covers vast areas of the south-west of the country. Although assistance was long ago withdrawn from these camps, neither these sites nor their people have ever been incorporated into the administration of the various offices responsible for local government in the area. They remained under the Ministry of Youth, Culture and Sports.

We might consider the Malawi example as a better model for integrating aid within government structures. Rather than replicating the work of the various ministries in isolation from them, Malawi has established a Task Force in which representatives of the concerned government offices (e.g., agriculture, health, education, and so on) jointly coordinate programmes of assistance to refugees that will ultimately be integrated into their economy. This model may avoid some of the pitfalls that have been experienced elsewhere (Karadawi, 1983; Harrell-Bond, 1986, chapter 2).

However, even if the Malawi government in this way is able to remain in control of policy and the expenditure of aid from outside, unless refugees and the local people among whom they live are also involved in planning, assistance programmes will still suffer the pernicious consequences of top-down planning (Chambers, 1983). Aid that is imposed from outside and from above usurps the roles of the hosts, suppresses the creative energy of refugees (who could have been helped to help themselves) and provokes responses that are hostile and unproductive for all concerned. Breaking the Monopoly of Power in Aid Provision or: How to Work as a Team Aid is a powerful tool of manipulation that has been delegated by donor governments to humanitarian agencies. The questions asked by agencies are: how much, what kind of aid, where, who, and when? What is never questioned is who should *make* these decisions. The failure to ask this question leads to misallocation of scarce resources, the misapplication of aid.

Standing as they do at this epicentre of political and economic power, the daily experiences of agency personnel or government officials continually confirm and reinforce their views - of themselves, of the helplessness of refugees, of the incapacity of local institutions and officials, and of the functions of aid distribution. As Pearse and Stiefel (1979) have noted, 'Although there are endless examples of directly repressive measures and acts against popular participation, it is the anti-participatory character of ideologies that provide the most persistent control as they mould attitudes and expectations of one group in relation to others.' If aid were to come from inside the host country, or if management responsibilities were shared with hosts and refugees, this power monopoly and ability to control the definition of the situation held by outsiders would be weakened.

The real hosts of refugees are the people in the locality in which they first arrive. Consider the following example of local level response to a refugee influx. When in 1983 refugees from Mozambique began entering Zimbabwe, the government first took a decision not to label them refugees. Dr Richard Laing, the medical officer for the district, together with his wife, a trained community worker, have described the response of the local community to this influx (Laing and Laing, 1986). The area concerned was some 150 miles from the Mozambique border.

When it first became obvious that there were abnormal numbers of people moving across the border, members of the local community, the agricultural officer, the district administrator and health officers discussed what should be done. Surveys were undertaken, letters and reports were sent to Harare and on one occasion two officials were flown to the area to talk about the problem. When the numbers grew, the first [unfortunate] official response was to order the police to pick up all the refugees and send them to a transit camp before repatriating them back to Mozambique. However the camp could only hold 5,000. By 10 o'clock on the day of the clean-up some 20,000 had been 'cleaned up'.

The next day the instructions came to take the people back to where they had been found. Local people began to mobilize to respond to the problem. The nearby hospital team came and vaccinated everyone. Local businessmen rounded up food and local citizens provided clothing.

So, when they were put back. . .they were in a terrible condition and everybody was highly concerned in that community. We all felt we must do something. We were all feeling very guilty about the fact that we were in comfort and they had nothing. . .I immediately recognized the need for some sort of power and in Africa. . .the power line is the men. We decided we would have to get some people with power in the community to form a committee. Our first committee consisted of the District Commissioner, his deputy, the head of the hospital, the Administrator of the hospital, the Matron, the church people, a bank manager and local businessmen. Basically, all these people were extremely busy but they were important because they represented the power in the community, the decision-making and they could make decisions

which the local people [could not]. The women, who were
doing some of the work, were unable to do. So we formed. .
this executive into the Bindura Mozambique Relief Committee and had the local bank do all the bookkeeping on a
voluntary basis. Our stocktaking was done by the local Administrator with his lock-up and security system. That was
very important because it gave us a feeling that things were
being monitored, any money...would not be abused. (Laing
and Laing, 1986)

It was explained to the refugees that, because the members
of the Management Committee were very busy, it was really
up to them to tell them what they wanted the Committee to
do. 'We are willing to help you if you let us know what your
needs are. You have to get yourselves organized into a
committee and decide what you need to do. . . .There was a
lot of discussion about what they thought was their need and
to elect leaders.'
     The details of the experiences of this local community
would be worth re-telling, but in short, everyone including
the local army and police got involved. Wherever possible
local resources were used, for example, a local traditional
high-protein drink made from roots was used in the feeding
programme for the children. Through experience, the local
committee learned how to break down mothers' fears of
reporting that their children were seriously ill. At all points,
the refugees were consulted and involved in sorting out
priorities and mobilizing their community to carry out the
work. As Mrs Laing put it:

When we started we had no experience of managing refugees, we knew nothing about refugees. . . .But our experience
of setting up primary health care programmes and within
primary health [showed] there are two sorts of approaches.
There is community supportive and community oppressive.
The community oppressive is very prescriptive saying this is
what you people must do, while the community supportive
tries to say we will support you in what you want to do. It

was with that background of experience that we came into the refugee organization or working with the community. . .I do not think we are saying anything against the big agencies. I think [they] have a role to play in getting the money, raising the money and getting the food down on the ground. But after that I think the people themselves could, through representation, decide how to use it the best. You see, even if they are not very good, I think they are still probably much better than an outsider could possibly be and that is the basic sort of underlying principle.

Towards a New Approach to Assisting the Uprooted

The Need for Research Training

In the full report of their experience in Zimbabwe, the Laings (1985) elaborate three major issues that inevitably confront all those involved in humanitarian assistance. The first is that upon which this paper has thus far concentrated: the 'politics' (micro and macro) that affect and are produced at each stage of the design, implementation and funding of programmes. Yet many of these political implications of aid provision are either not acknowledged or seen to be secondary problems, quite residual in comparison to the 'practical' demands of everyday aid-giving. The second is how profoundly lack of information and misinformation affects what aid is, and is not. The Laings describe, in great detail, the mistakes they made because they lacked crucial information concerning the characteristics of the people they were trying to help. They sometimes act on premises that are later found to be wrong.

Their report shows the value of involving the refugees themselves in the collection of information to guide practice, but to be efficient, a participatory approach to research needs to be more systematic. Thirdly, although the Laings brought relevant training from the field of public health that was based on a 'community supportive' rather than a 'community oppressive' approach, they had 'no experience in managing refugees, we knew nothing about refugees'. There is obviously a need for people who work with refugees to be trained in appropriate methods of aid provision and for that training to be informed by independent research. As Chambers (1986) has noted, 'Despite the scale and the awfulness of...forced mass migrations, there has been little systematic study of...refugee relief work in Africa or indeed elsewhere. Until recently, refugee studies itself has not been recognized as a subject.'

The particular challenge of the study of forced migration is that it requires coherent and integrated research strategies that incorporate the knowledge, methods, theories and concepts of a number of disciplines and to be responsive to the needs of practitioners. It is not that 'research' on some refugee issues is all that rare. Rather, it is that most of it is conducted 'in-house' by aid agencies or contracted by them. Pehaps the chief problem with this kind of research is that it almost of necessity (consciously or unconsciously) reflects the priorities and world-view of the very programmes and procedures that are so much in need of change. As Mazur (1988) observes: 'Reports of agencies' field staff, particularly those that are critical, would be an important source of insights concerning existing practices were they not kept out of the public realm' (Harrell-Bond, 198, p. 314).

The Need for Independent Research

Researchers must be able to maintain independence if they are to do critical work, and this is difficult in situations where most of the funding available for refugee research (and even access to refugees) is controlled by governments or other sources that serve their interest. With some very few exceptions, the majority of research that has been conducted on refugees in Africa has been done as short-term consultancies 'rather than independent, sustained sociological efforts.

Serious questions arise as to whether consultancies provide a format in which existing assumptions are critically evaluated and new concepts are developed' (Mazur, 1988).

Unless the consultant is an established scholar with long experience of a people and an area, it is unlikely that useful findings will result. The short-term nature of most consultancies and the limits of the terms of reference of such assignments mean that rarely will a researcher have time actually to study the community concerned. Most consultants rely almost entirely on guided tours, interviews and documents available in the country rather than actually conducting field research that ensures that the points of view and experience of refugees themselves and their immediate hosts are represented in their findings. The terms of most contracts include the requirement that the researcher sign away his or her independence by promising not to publish. If research does not find its way into the public domain, there is no accountability. The organization funding the research may simply shelve the results. The temptation to avoid criticism, however constructive, is great for the consultant when economic survival depends on this source of employment.

The Weakness of Present Refugee Research

Even those social scientists, using predominantly positivist epistemologies, are not likely to examine their own assumptions critically in order to understand the diverse circumstances faced by refugees and their hosts or the abilities of refugees to reconstruct their own lives.

Few utilize genuinely participatory research methods that will enable 'outsiders' to comprehend the refugees' perspective on problems and solutions. Ultimately, issues of control, central to the sociology of knowledge and information, must be addressed (Mazur, 1988).

There are two basic ways in which refugee studies research in general can become more sophisticated, more accurate, and more aware of its philosophical biases. One way is to encourage more research by individuals and groups who are 'outsiders' to the system they investigate; I will have much more to say about this shortly. The other is to increase refugee input to research, both directly through their own research and through the development of research orientations that 'bring the people back in' to research that is now chiefly statistical.

Participation has become a buzz word in development circles. However, as Mark Malloch-Brown noted, 'Refugee work remains, perhaps, the last bastion of the ultra-paternalistic approach to aid and development. It is hard to think of another area where the blinkered nonsense of the "We know what's best for them" approach survives so unchallenged' (1984). Chambers (1987) believes that the neglect of involving refugees in administration of their own communities, in identifying their own needs and in gathering information that aid givers require is largely due to the images of the helpless refugees created by the media and used by agencies to raise funds. However, as he points out, refugees 'usually have a great capacity for active self-help, given the chance'.

Participation is about empowering the poor to take control of their own lives, about being able to involve themselves effectively in decision-making. At a minimum this requires providing the means to acquire access to information and providing opportunities for people to examine both the external forces that oppress them as well as their own values and beliefs that condition their own responses. Only then can the poor begin to devise strategies to combat the forces that oppress them.

A study conducted with Ugandan refugees in southern Sudan (Harrell-Bond, 1986) provides a case in point. The research was planned to allow refugees to participate both in the analysis of their situation and in conveying their views about the aid programme in question. In each settlement, refugees were provided information on how the aid they were receiving was organized, its limitations and what they could legitimately expect. They were told which agencies were involved, and what were their rights and duties in relation to the assistance programme and the host government. It should be noted that even such basic information as what items the World Food Programme rations were intended to comprise, where it originated and who was responsible for its delivery and distribution had never been provided. (Little wonder when, as so regularly was the case, supplies did not arrive - in this case all the way from Mombasa by lorry through war-torn Uganda - the refugees accused their hosts of mismanagement and corruption.) Refugee participation in this research project profoundly affected the assistance programme in southern Sudan and also provided a significant challenge to the aid-giving status quo in the region. Perhaps most importantly, it had an impact on the refugee community itself. One tangible outcome was the building of a self-help secondary school in co-operation with the local Sudanese.

Let us consider another way in which research might be expanded. There is an urgent need for experienced scholars to turn their attention to the study of all aspects of forced migration and to establish a basis for co-operation between themselves, governments, and the humanitarian agencies that provide assistance to refugees. If solutions are to be found to this pressing humanitarian problem, further research is imperative in order that the general public, as well as governments, can come to a clearer understanding of the fundamental causes of forced migration and the issues facing all those involved.[3] Moreover, it is necessary to recognize that at present few opportunities exist for practitioners, refugees and researchers to meet and work together, and that there is a serious understanding gap between each and the other two. Practitioners consider outside 'academics' either to be a threat or (worse still!) irrelevant; university-based academics too easily discount the everyday difficulties and constraints faced by aid workers; refugees are frustrated by their lack of input into programmes deeply

affecting them. It is only through 'working together separately', remaining primarily practitioners, academics, refugees, and yet cross-fertilizing each other's understandings -
that these unwarranted barriers can be reduced.

Constraints on Research

Many government officials and agency staff still need to be
convinced of the value of research to inform practice. It is, I
think, one of our weaknesses that we have not yet developed
the resources, the communications skills, or sufficient trust
to gain the full confidence of international aid agencies.
There is another major constraint on research, and its utilization. Chambers has observed that there are presently far too
few researchers in the world who have access to, and understanding of, the rich and detailed system of knowledge of the
poor, and that these comparatively few do not influence development so long as practitioners continue to be conditioned to despise that knowledge (1983, p. 84). It may well be
that participatory research methods (which include them in
the process) based on a wide-ranging view of refugees and
their contexts may be the best way to do this.
    There are other challenges too. As Indra (1988) has
noted, refugees everywhere in the world amost always
share one characteristic: they are rarely addressed as multidimensional children, men and women who happen to be
refugees, but rather as a set of social problems.

> Public concern, policy, programming, the media are all
> chiefly involved with things which concern refugees and are
> seen to be problematic: the conditions which create refugees,
> flight, camp life, finding jobs and all the other integration
> issues. This derives in part from the media accenting refu-
> gees as a social issue by applying to them the conventional
> grid of what is news, which is chiefly problematic. The
> reasons why refugees thereafter become legitimate social
> issues are complex, but centrally they include the necessity of

helping bureaucracies, governments and advocacy groups
to define refugees within a charter of crisis and social need.
(Ibid.)

There are a number of consequences that follow defining
refugees as 'a problem'. It is easier to mobilize social concern
on easily conceptualized and simplified issues and through
appealing to such motives as 'guilt' to raise funds. It allows,
as we have seen, bureaucracies to extend their spheres of
influence and to legitimize their involvement. It provides the
justification for creating new institutions of assistance. By
putting a social problem orientation on to refugee issues, it
is possible to conceal the 'explicitly political nature of interest group actions. . . .It does this through several ways. . .
Centrally, it does this through the implicit claim that such
identified "social problems" are grounded on non-contro-
versial, non-negotiable societal values, and hence are not
political' (ibid.)

What is of concern is how this social problem approach
to the study of refugees organizes relations between them
and others, how it marginalizes refugees and maintains a
separation between them and others. As Indra observes, this
approach has an impact on the refugees themselves by
organizing the individual refugee's orientation in terms of
his or her 'problems'. Most important, such research's applied
value is weakened inasmuch as there is no guarantee that it
is concentrated either on what are the most important social
issues, either objectively or from the refugees' point of view.

There are a number of reasons why this kind of
research tends to be very non-reflective about its own nature
- something we are trying to fight. Indra points out that a
'social problem' orientation limits the depth to which research can detach itself from what it is investigating - from
the manifest functions of organizations, from their voiced
priorities for social assistance, from the implicit assumptions
that these priorities are, if not the most central, at least
important. It also makes a shambles of any attempt to

explain policy making, inasmuch as such an analysis far too often takes literally government, social service, and agency statements of purpose. It depoliticizes analysis by speaking of 'effective' or 'ineffective' programme decisions, but not of the political determinants and consequences of those decisions. It fails to address how individuals, groups, and institutions use social problem arguments concerning refugees to advance their interests, to grow, to counter other social problem claims, to cut themselves off from external review, to isolate themselves from contradictory definitions of the situation developed by 'outsiders'.

It is with social problem research, as with aid: most groups of refugees receive research attention when they are in high relief as 'social problems'. When they fade from view, research fades also.

We need to develop refugee studies as a more coherent field of research than it is at present. Reflecting its nature as a new field, those who participate in it come from a wide range of disciplinary and topical backgrounds. They often come to refugee studies without prior experience in the field, only to leave it after a project or two. The pervasive social problem orientation itself magnifies these tendencies. Lacking a disciplinary core to ground research, there is also a very strong tendency to 'particularize' the research on a given refugee group. Thus there is little comparative refugee research in specific countries and little reference to findings on specific refugee groups who are living in different countries.

The lack of a refugee studies paradigm and the present social problem concentration conspires together to cut 'the heart out of the refugee experience' by not allowing much significance to a wide range of phenomena worthy of research and to *kinds* of research. For example, it slights in-depth anthropological research *vis-à-vis* quantitative survey research.

Thus, even some of the most sensitive and multidimensional aspects of refugee life such as mental health are discussed on the basis of data collected through one-time surveys administered to people who have never had experience of this kind of inquiry.

Independent studies are urgently needed that are based upon field research rather than relying only on 'expert' inteviews and existing public documents produced by agencies. Academics who write about refugees too often adopt terms that are employed by agencies as concepts without carefully defining them. There is a tendency to place uncritical reliance on official literature as sources without actually studying refugee situations.

Key Issues for Future Study

There are, of course, a host of topical issues concerning Africa and refugees that require far greater research attention, and these will be identified briefly here.

1. *Causes of refugee flows*
Little systematic work has been devoted to understanding the structural context of Africa's refugee exoduses. While cursory attention has been paid repeatedly to the effects of the artificial partitioning of Africa, the specific impact of policies and practices institutionalized under colonial rule and their contemporary legacy have not been the object of in-depth analysis (Mazur, 1988). The issues of ethnic conflict that underlies many refugee-producing situations require far greater attention than scholars have thus far given them. So also does practical working out of the processes of nation-building and their effect on refugee flight.

2. *Repatriation*
Eventual repatriation is increasingly championed by UNHCR and others as the 'durable solution' of first choice. It is seen as appropriate that refugees should return to their home country once the immediate cause of flight has disappeared. It is also assumed that once refugees have returned to their

home country, only short-term relief programmes are required to facilitate their economic reintegration. How true is this? Studies are needed that examine what happens when people go home. What factors affect their welcome? How is reintegration into the country of origin affected by experiences in asylum (eg. experiences of assistance in camp, skills training and employment experience, education of children, and so on). How is it affected by the fact that the country itself will have changed while they were away? If refugee reintegration is to be achieved without engendering further significant dislocation, a good deal of research needs to be done on matters affecting reintegration.

3. Ecological issues

As most assistance programmes are designed for the short-term, it is only recently that aid-givers have begun to pay attention to the massive impact on the ecology that results from refugee flight, influxes, and long-term settlement in host countries. Research on these issues is immediately relevant to decisions on day-to-day policy and programming, and would help to avoid situations where, for example, refugees have severely depleted natural resources as a result of the need for fuel, building materials or grazing land for their animals.

4. Motivational issues

Surprisingly little theoretical and empirical research has been done on individual-level motivations and flight decisions: whether, when, and how to flee, where to go, etc. Delineating these factors influencing refugees' exodus implicitly presumes the achievement of an underlying understanding, or operational model of decision-making. Viewed this way, refugees (like other migrants) are seen as individuals who plan, weigh alternatives, and choose rationally, rather than just as pawns in a larger game. Further, they may in this way be studied in regard to how their previously learned skills are used in strategic decision-making to improve status and well-being in their new location.

5. *Gender issues*

It is often the case that women outnumber men in refugee situations. However, wherever research has been conducted it appears that there is very little acknowledgement that men and women may be very differently situated in the refugee process. Male domination is a feature of most societies (inluding those of the aid community), and assistance programmes are usually 'gender blind'. They do not distinguish between men and women refugees. The failure to recognize women's pivotal position in the household economy of many refugee groups or their special needs in refugee situations has already led to women being disadvantaged and to whole programmes going awry. We live in a genderized world. Research should reflect this and always be disaggregated in respect to gender.

6. *Socialization, educational and enculturation issues*

Actions by refugees have been labelled by aidworkers and other commentators as 'conservative' - implying an absence of adaptability and a persistent attempt on their part to maintain their social, economic and cultural characteristics and institutions under conditions of stress (Oliver-Smith and Hansen, 1982, p. 3; Scudder and Colson, 1982). Refugees may attempt to cling to the familiar and change no more than is necessary in order to reduce any further stress. Yet such ideas also imply active struggles by refugees. It is certain that many refugees do return to a life that is outward-looking and characterized by initiative and risk-taking, though this aspect is poorly researched. It is known, at least, that when refugees actively participate in the reconstruction of their environment, they re-establish the increasing positive self-image necessary for genuine development. Further, it is everywhere presumed that refugees wish, and in some psychological way need to re-establish familiar institutions

and symbols by relocating with kin, neighbours and co-
ethnics to create some sense of 'community'. Unfortunately,
the resources and subtle processes involved in re-establish-
ing these bases of social and economic life have been little
researched. Neither have the re-establishment of institutions to perpetuate cultural traditions and socialization.
How are familial, camp- and community-based institutions
established (if at all) to maintain cultural traditions and
transmit them to the young? How do these institutions and
their cultural load change because of the refugee experience?
How are socialization mechanisms and informal systems of
social control established? How are all of these affected by
new 'imposed' or self-created institutions of education,
social control and the like? Almost nothing is as yet known
in detail of any of these, yet both repatriation and host
country settlement are based on premises that this cultural
and social core exists, and that it is the primary basis for the
re-establishment of a normal social life.

In a more technical vein, it is obvious that flight always
disrupts people's economic and educational pursuits. It is
generally acknowledged that education is a high priority
among African refugees and that they will, if it is possible,
put a great deal of energy into building up their own
educational facilities. More research needs to be done on
how external programmes for training and for the education
of refugees can better tap these deep aspirations for education.

*7. Issues of economic, social and political integration into host
societies*
As has been noted, most refugees in Africa are in self-settled
rural areas rather than in camps. Large numbers of unassisted refugees are also living in the towns and cities of their
host country. One study (Kuhlman et al., 1987) has already
presented a case where such urban refugees make a positive
contribution to the economy of the host, do not drive up the
costs of rent (as was believed), and provide a cheap, docile

labour force that benefits some sections of the population without producing much direct competition with local people for jobs. Only further research can establish whether this is a general pattern and where potential mutual benefits and potential conflicts exist between hosts and refugees. Unassisted refugees can be and are incorporated into the local political order or they may have a major impact upon local power relations (Wilson et al., 1985). More work needs to be done on grass-roots questions of social control and support structures.

8. *Issues of resettlement*

Both the United States and Canada have an annual quota for African refugees that tends to be 'filled' with higher class applicants from the Horn of Africa. There is considerable controversy over the issue of resettlement. Different points of view are held concerning resettlement within the receiving country, by host governments, by refugee organizations, and by the refugees themselves. While the resettlement of African refugees in such rich countries is likely to remain a minor 'solution', this does not mean that programmes of resettlement have no impact in source and host countries. Remittances may affect local economies. Competition for resettlement may create relative refugee and host deprivation. Programmes to select individuals for resettlement may challenge host country (and refugee organization) autonomy. Most of these issues have not yet been researched.

9. *Psycho-social issues*

A refugee's predicament is not one that can ever be fully 'solved'. As is the case with all profound human experiences, those traumas and changes in life circumstances that uprooted people undergo may always have some bearing on their psychological health as well as on their social relations in whatever community they live. Life in exile may mean that a person lives in a state of permanent objective social alienation. It may also mean that they suffer serious psycho-social problems that are the result of a loss of grounded personal situation, community and culture that are not satisfactorily reconstituted among strangers. On the other hand, the necessity to adjust to an alien culture may constitute an optimum condition for the release of enormous creative energy (Jonas, 1988; Eisenbruch, 1988).

As Berry (1987) noted, 'Up until a decade ago, very little was known about the [psychological] factors which appear to operate when people move between cultures.' Now, however, there is a body of literature that indicates that there are sometimes serious mental health consequences. It has been demonstrated that these are likely to be more serious for people who are not in voluntary contact with another culture or who have not migrated voluntarily (e.g., Rack, 1982: 150-9; Baker, 1983; Berry, 1987; Eisenbruch, 1988). Furthermore, in many countries in which they finally settle, refugees are among the most powerless of minority groups *vis-à-vis* the dominant culture. Some individuals have suffered imprisonment and torture, or have witnessed the death (often violent) of family and friends. Presumably both of these compound refugee psychological problems.

These observations lead to many deep and compelling research questions. What is the prevalence of mental health problems among refugee populations? So far, we know this in detail only for south-east Asians in North America. Who in a given group (re. gender, age, generation, and personal situation) is more likely to experience these problems? How and to what degree do these mental difficulties affect people's social and economic lives? How significantly does the re-establishment of a rewarding personal economic situation, a family and culture mitigate these problems? All demand further research.

10. *Children*
The OAU declared 1988 as the year of the African Child. The tragedy is that so many African children spent that year and will spend many subsequent ones in flight, in refugee camps,

and in the uncertainties of resettlement. UNICEF and other agencies do have important programmes to meet the physical needs of children, but these have not yet been able to adequately address the particular needs of refugee children, many of whom have lost the stability of home, or have seen close kin killed or otherwise brutalized. There is a good deal of evidence from research in Europe and America that children who have suffered mistreatment grow up to mistreat others, and so a deadly cycle is established. The conditions that create refugees also create a generation of children who can become those who in their own time torment others.

We need research programmes that look directly at what is happening to those of Africa's children who are being subjected to the turmoils of displacement, pinpoint their needs, and then help produce programmes that give them reassurance that basic human values still exist, and remain necessary if they and others are to have a decent human life. Such research would also help in the development of programmes to assist these children to cope with the past and build towards the future.

Notes

[1] This chapter is based upon results from the research, practical experience of (and discussions with) a great many people - especially those refugees, students, African government officials, UNHCR and other agency staff members, field practitioners and academics - who have been part of the Refugee Studies Programme or who have participated in courses and seminars at Oxford since the Programme began in 1982. It has not always been possible to credit them as they deserve. Dr Robert Mazur (1988) was commissioned by the RSP to write a paper which outlined the 'state of the art' in sociological studies of refugees in Africa and I have drawn extensively on his work. My major intellectual debt as far as understanding refugee issues is concerned is to Ahmed Karadawi, upon whose research and

long experience in refugee assistance in the Sudan many at the RSP depend for inspiration. I also wish to thank Professor Elizabeth Colson who has recently joined the Refugee Studies Programme, for helping me to decide what aspects of such a complicated issue as forced migration should be covered in this chapter. I particularly wish to note the substantive as well as editorial assistance I have had from both Dr Doreen Indra and Dr Norman Buchignani, Visiting Research Fellows with the RSP. Both are anthropologists who have brought a rich background of research in race relations, ethnic studies, public policy and gender issues to the study of refugee issues. Their presence in the RSP has greatly increased our awareness of the need to contextualize studies of refugee issues within the existing theoretical literature.

[2] The Refugee Studies Programme (RSP) was established at the University of Oxford in 1982.

[3] RSP at Oxford sees no contradiction between research being scholarly and doing it to influence policy. It seeks to carry out independent, interdisciplinary research of concrete refugee situations leading to general theoretical models of refugee flows and refugee assistance, and to develop better methods to evaluate assistance programmes and policies. I believe that the RSP is unique in its emphasis on encouraging the establishment of refugee studies in host countries and promoting an international network of institutions involved in research, training, and documentation. A *Directory of Current Refugee Research,* which is updated annually, and a new *Journal of Refugee Studies* are produced to promote collaboration among researchers who previously had been working in isolation. The RSP has also established the *Refugee Participation Network* , to disseminate research findings to practitioners and to provide a means of communication between them and researchers with the aim of improving the delivery of assistance in the field. One objective of the Refugee Studies Programme at Oxford is to encourage African academics to develop the skills to research (and teach) refugee issues.

References

Cernea, M. M. (1988), *Involuntary Resettlement in Development Projects: Policy Guidelines in World Bank-Financed Projects*, Washington, DC: World Bank.

Chambers, R. (1986), 'Hidden Losers? The Impact of Rural Refugees and Refugee Programs on Poorer Hosts', *International Migration Review*, XX, 2, 1986.

Colson, E. and Scudder, T. (1982), 'From Welfare to Development: A Conceptual Framework for the Analysis of Dislocated People', in A. Hansen and A. Oliver-Smith (eds), *Involuntary Migration and Resettlement: the Problems and Responses of Dislocated People*, pp. 267-88.

Colson, E. (1982), 'Planned Change: The Creation of a New Community', Institute of International Studies, University of California, Berkeley. Reprinted in *Refugee Participation Network Newsletter*, 2, May 1988.

Crisp, J. (1984), 'Voluntary Repatriation Programmes for African Refugees: A Critical Examination', *Refugee Issues*, 1, 2, December.

Davidson, B. (1988), 'Storm in the Horn of Famine', *The Guardian*, Monday 13 June.

Dunbar-Ortiz, R. and Harrell-Bond, B. (1987), 'Who Protects the Human Rights of Refugees?', *Africa Today: Human Rights: the African Context*, 34, 1 & 2, pp. 105-25.

Hansen, A. (1979), 'Once the Running Stops: Assimilation of Angolan Refugees into Zambian Border Villages', *Disasters*, 3 April, pp. 369-74.

Hansen, A. and Oliver-Smith, A. (eds) (1982), *Involuntary Migration Resettlement: The Problems and Responses of Dislocated People*, Boulder, Colorado: Westview Press.

Harrell-Bond, B., Howard, A. and Skinner, D. (1978) *Community Leadership and the Transformation of Freetown 1801-1976*, The Hague: Mouton.

Harrell-Bond, B. and Karadawi, A. (1984), 'Giving Refugees a Voice'. A Report of the International Symposium 'Assistance to Refugees: Alternative Viewpoints', *Disasters*, 8 April.

Harrell-Bond, B. (1986), *Imposing Aid: Emergency Assistance to Refugees*, Oxford: Oxford University Press.

Harrell-Bond, B. and Kanyeihamba, G. (1987), 'Improving the Standards of Human Rights and Refugee Protection in Africa', *Disasters*, 6, 4, May.

Harrell-Bond, B. (1988), 'Repatriation: Under What Conditions is it the Most Desirable Solution for Refugees?', unpublished ms.

Hocke, J. P. (1986), 'Beyond Humanitarianism: The Need for Political Will to Resolve Today's Refugee Problem', RSP Joyce Pearce Memorial Lecture delivered 29 October at Oxford University.

Indra, D. (1988), 'One Key Issue Concerning Refugees and Resettlement', discussion paper delivered to the Refugee Studies Programme, Oxford University, June.

Jaeger, G. (1988), Lecture Series, Refugee Studies Programme, Hilary Term.

Karadawi, A. (1983), 'Constraints on Assistance to Refugees: Some Observations from the Sudan', *World Development*, 11, 6, pp. 537-47.

Karadawi et al. (1987), 'The Social Problems of Development', The Other Economic Summit, background papers for the first Libreville Summit, January 26-8, prepared by The Other Economic Summit (TOES), at the request of Association Mondiale de Prospective Sociale (AMPS).

Kibreab, G. (1983), *Reflections of the African Refugee Problem: A Critical Analysis of Some Basic Assumptions*, Research Report 67, Scandinavian Institute of African Studies, Uppsala.

Kibreab, G. (November 1987), 'How Durable are the "Durable Solutions" to the Problem of African Refugees?', overview paper for the Refugee Research Workshop, Nairobi 14-17 December. University of Uppsala, Sweden.

Kursany, I. (1985), 'Eritrean Refugees in Kassala Province of Eastern Sudan: An Economic Assessment', *Refugee Issues*, 2, 1, October.

Laing, R. (1987), 'The Role of Voluntary Agencies in Development: A Recipients' Perspective?', paper presented to RSP/Queen Elizabeth House Conference, December.

Laing, R. and Mrs Laing (1986), 'Crisis Management in Zimbabwe', seminar paper, Refugee Studies Programme, Research Class, 9 June.

Lusk, G. (1988), 'Refugees of War Get Poor Welcome', *The Guardian*, Monday 13 June.

Malloch-Brown, M. (1984), as quoted in Harrell-Bond and Karadawi, *Disasters*, 8 May, p. 254.

Mazur, R. (1988), 'Refugees in Africa: The Role of Sociological Analysis and Praxis', *Current Sociology: The Sociology of Forced Migration*.

Morss, E. (1984), 'Institutional Destruction Resulting from Donor and Project Proliferation in the Sub-Saharan Countries', *World Development*, 12, 4, pp. 465-70.

Pearse, A. and Stiefel, M. (1979), 'Inquiry into Participation: A Research Approach', Geneva: UNRISD.

Rizvi, Zia (1984), as quoted in Harrell-Bond and Karadawi, *Disasters*, 8 April.

Salinas, M., Pritchard, D. and Kibedi, A. (1987), 'Refugee-Based Organisations: Their Function and Importance for the Refugee in Britain', in *Refugee Issues*, 3, 4, July.

Shacknove, A. E. (1985), 'Who is a Refugee?', *Ethics*, 95, 2, January.

Tandon, Y. (1987), 'Some Disturbing Trends in the African and International Refugees Situation and the Way Forward', presented at the 'Refugee Workers Awareness Building/Communicators' Seminar', organized for Anglophone African Countries by the All Africa Conference of Churches in Mombasa, Kenya, in September.

Waldron, S. R. (1987), 'Blaming the Refugees', *Refugee Issues*, 3, 3, April.

Wilson, K. B., McGregor, J., Wright, J., Myers, M., de Waal, A. and Pankhurst, A. (1985), *The Lutaya Expedition: A Report on Research in Yei River District*, Refugee Studies Occasional Paper, 1.

Woodford, T. (1988), 'UN Refugee Magazine is Burnt "to Appease the West Germans"', *The Guardian*, 8 January.

Zetter, R. (1987), 'Rehousing the Greek-Cypriot Refugees from 1974: A Study of Institutional Access and Labelling', unpublished D.Phil thesis: University of Sussex, May.

Zetter, R. (1988), 'Report of Visit to Malawi, Zambia and Zimbabwe Refugee Studies Programme, Oxford University, June.

Appendix
Resolutions and Recommendations from the International Symposium 'Assistance to Refugees: Alternative Viewpoints'

Resolutions of the Symposium

1. The Symposium calls upon the international community to address itself urgently and seriously to the root causes of refugee exoduses; to take the measures necessary to obviate further refugee exoduses, and facilitate the return of refugees to their country of origin if and when they wish to do so. The Symposium calls upon the international community to examine the pressures that can be brought to bear on governments that provoke refugee exoduses. The members of the Symposium express their commitment to the cause of refugees and oppressed peoples, and call on all other individuals to work towards the goal of a world without refugees.

2. The Symposium welcomes the commitment of African governments to instruments such as the United Nations Universal Declaration of Human Rights and OAU Convention on Refugees, and welcomes the decision of the Organization of African Unity to establish an African Commission on Human Rights. The Symposium calls on all African governments to remove the conditions which create refugees and to protect existing refugees by observing the provisions of these instruments, above all by observing the principle of non-refoulement. The Symposium also calls on all African governments to make every effort to resolve national conflicts and protect minorities.

3. The Symposium recognizes the important financial contribution of those countries which give assistance to refugees in Africa,

urges those countries to increase their contributions, and calls on all countries currently not making such contributions to do so. The Symposium calls on all countries to desist from the pursuit of any political, economic, or military policy that creates or perpetuates the conditions that provoke refugee exoduses in Africa and elsewhere.

4. The Symposium calls on the UNHCR, host governments, donor governments and NGOs urgently to promote the participation of refugees in all decision-making structures and procedures affecting their conditions of life.

(i) At the local level, this would involve an obligation on the part of the UNHCR, host governments, donor governments and NGOs to develop appropriate fora and procedures for refugee participation in decision-making and in the monitoring of local expenditures on refugees. This obligation should be reflected in the text of implementing agreements.

(ii) At the national level, existing refugee organizations should be recognized and involved in policy-making procedures on relevant issues. This would include the vetting of implementing partners, and monitoring the extent to which money raised in the name of the refugees is spent on refugees. Where refugee organizations do not exist or where they are not fully representative, other forms of refugee participation should be facilitated.

(iii) At the international level, efforts should be made to find ways to allow refugee participation in relevant structures and procedures, without compromising the humanitarian, non-political status of host countries.

(iv) The Symposium urges the UNHCR, NGOs and host governments to employ refugees.

(v) Above all, refugees must participate in any decision concerning voluntary repatriation.

Recommendations of the Symposium

1. *Economic Development*

The Symposium recommends:
1.1 That refugees and refugee communities be enabled to become economically self-reliant as quickly as possible. The Symposium

therefore welcomes the UNHCR's report on Refugee Aid and Development, and calls on the international community to provide the resources that would enable its recommendations to be implemented.

1.2 That relevant bodies place greater emphasis on allowing refugees and refugee organizations to administer development funds and projects.

1.3 That where integrated development plans are introduced, equal access to the available resources is guaranteed for refugees.

1.4 That where refugees are leaving a country in which civil war or liberation struggle is taking place, development funds be made available for areas not under the control of the central government in order to prevent or reduce the outflow of refugees from that area.

2. *Education and Training*

The Symposium recommends:

2.1 That educational programmes for refugees, including vocational training, be prepared with regard to the fact that refugees come from diverse backgrounds and into different situations. They cannot, therefore, be treated as a single unit.

2.2 That relevant organizations aim to provide a balance in educational provisions for refugees, allocating scarce resources between non-formal, primary, secondary, vocational and further education sectors in accordance with the specific needs of each situation.

2.3 That in the light of the above recommendations, educational liaison committees be established in each host country, bringing together refugee representatives, relevant NGOs, UNHCR staff and Education Ministry officials, to formulate appropriate educational policies and practices.

2.4 That information on all aspects of education be urgently made available to all refugees through the development of refugee educational counselling services, [staffed] by professionally qualified staff with appropriate information relevant to all levels of education.

2.5 That a system of examination, assessment and certification be devised for implementation by the UNHCR and local Ministries of Education, which will be equivalent in standard across countries, which will be recognized by governments and academic institutions, and which will provide better access to education to refugees without certificates and documents.

2.6 That the UNHCR, relevant NGOs and host governments give much greater emphasis to non-formal modes of education in view of the fact that it affects the largest number of refugees, including the majority of refugee women.

2.7 That within the area of non-formal education, special attention be paid to the development of projects organized by refugees, and to the training and proper payment of non-formal educators. Non-formal education (distance teaching, radio broadcasts, village class, home and community teaching) must also be used to teach refugees in areas such as health, agriculture, child-care, nutrition, hygiene and practical skills such as sewing, weaving and pottery.

2.8 That vocational training programmes for refugees be devised only after a careful study of job opportunities in both host and home countries.

2.9 That vocational training be linked to productive work, and that agencies sponsoring such training assist refugees to find their first job through the provision of equipment, advice, introductions and temporary material support.

2.10 That the search for a larger number of appropriate educational opportunities and bursaries for refugees at post-secondary level be intensified, and that students and placements be selected by professionally qualified panels and with regard to future employment opportunities.

2.11 That refugee education policy always be developed with regard to the host country's educational policy, in order to optimize the use of resources for the good of both refugees and the host community.

2.12 That as refugee education is preferably integrated into the national education system of the host country, instruction will be in the language of the host country. If this is the case, however, refugees require two special provisions: first, that extra language training be provided; and second, that additional classes to maintain the refugees' own language and background also be given.

3. *Health*

The main health problems in refugee settlement areas are brought about by failures in public health. The Symposium therefore recommends:

3.1 That a strong emphasis be placed on preventative health care without removing refugees' rights to receive adequate curative care.

3.2 That primary health care be implemented in refugee settlements in line with the host government's policy, and that health facilities be provided where they do not exist for both refugees and the host community.

3.3 That the UNHCR mandate be re-examined so that it is able to provide health and other forms of assistance to internally displaced people.

3.4 That the host governments and implementing partners increase their efforts to employ suitably qualified refugees in their refugee health programmes, and that refugees be trained in the prevention and treatment of common diseases.

3.5 That the UNHCR co-ordinate and support programmes in the areas of countries that are likely to host a refugee influx, and train personnel and prepare contingency plans so as to effect a rapid response to refugee emergencies.

3.6 That greater co-ordination be achieved in the health programmes of different agencies operational in the same area. That the drugs used are only those recommended by the UNHCR and World Health Organization. That greater efforts be made to monitor the standards and success of such programmes.

3.7 That greater access to relevant research be provided to refugee health workers. That further research be conducted into the provision of health care to urban refugees and into health care generally.

4. *The Media*

The refugee situation is regrettably one of the most dramatic in Africa today. The Symposium recommends:

4.1 That the media make a much greater effort to understand this situation, of which the traditional image of starving children is but a caricature.

4.2 That all those involved in refugee situations recognize the importance of a partnership with the media. Equally, the media must recognize its responsibility to publicize the plight of refugees. This is often essential to their security. NGOs must actively seek to inform the media in their home countries on the refugee issue.

4.3 That the media are encouraged to understand the political and economic contexts of refugee situations and the ability of refugees to play a substantial part in the management of their affairs. Refugee self-help is a better story than the usual one of helpless dependency.

4.4 That refugees be encouraged to gain experience in dealing with the media, and to supply the media with more and better information.

4.5 That the right of refugees to information and communication services be formally recognized in the international instruments governing the status and conditions of refugees.

4.6 That within refugee settlement areas, efforts be made to ensure that no single group of refugees has control of these information and communication services.

4.7 That host governments be encouraged to give journalists free access to refugee communities within their countries.

4.8 That the local media in host countries be encouraged to give coverage to refugee issues and to allow the refugees' voices to be heard.

5. *Protection*

The Symposium recommends:

5.1 That all countries which have not yet acceded to the relevant international legal instruments on the subject of refugee protection be urged to do so at an early date.

5.2 That countries which have acceded to the relevant instruments re-examine any reservations which they may have made at the date of accession or subsequently, with a view to the lifting of such reservations, and to review any relevant national legislation for the same purpose.

5.3 That the UNHCR be actively involved in the monitoring of the protection offered to refugees by host governments and insist on the granting of refugee status to all those eligible.

5.4 That identity cards and other necessary documents be issued as a matter of course to all refugees at an early date following their arrival in the country of asylum. That funding be made available for such documents, and that all information obtained in the registration process remain confidential and not divulged to the country of origin. That in no circumstances should refugees incur expenses in connection with the registration and documentation process.

5.5 That the rights and duties contained in any relevant legislation be made known to all persons affected, including refugees, members of the host community, and officials of the host government - particularly those in the police and immigration services.

5.6 That consideration be given by the responsible parties to the development of appropriate methods of encouraging the absorption of the concept and context of refugee rights into the ethics of the host community.

5.7 That all UNHCR staff members be adequately trained and equipped to handle protection issues.

5.8 That the international community strongly condemn the recent occurrence (in flagrant violation of international law and human morality) of the refoulement of refugees in East Africa, involving Kenya, Tanzania and Uganda. That the international community give urgent attention to the present position of these refugees, addressing itself to every means of alleviating their plights. That the international community consider appropriate methods of strengthening the machinery for the international protection of refugees, in particular, methods aimed at the prevention of such incidents and the possibility of imposing sanctions following contraventions of the fundamental legal principle of non-refoulement.

5.9 That all countries adopt a more liberal policy in connection with the granting of asylum, in particular, those European countries which had introduced legal or administrative barriers to the granting of asylum.

5.10 That NGOs and the UNHCR strengthen their co-operation in every aspect of refugee protection.

5.11 That host governments be helped by the international community to resist military incursions designed to weaken or violate the protection of refugees.

6. *Repatriation*

The Symposium recommends:
6.1 That voluntary repatriation be a decision taken by the refugee alone. The role of UNHCR is to provide information which will help the refugee arrive at that decision. Fact-finding missions undertaken by refugee leaders are an important part of this information-gathering process.
6.2 That only when the decision to repatriate is taken should the UNHCR and governments concerned effect arrangements for the return. In particular, the UNHCR should not make formal arrangements without consulting refugees and where there has been no major political change in the country of origin.
6.3 That neutral observers from bodies concerned with human rights be involved in the assessment of the situation in a country of origin and that these observers monitor the whole process of voluntary repatriation.
6.4 That the UNHCR introduce appropriate methods of verifying the safety and protection of refugees who have voluntarily returned to their countries of origin.
6.5 That in the light of these recommendations, the UNHCR refrain from entering into further tripartite arrangements such as those governing the process of repatriation from Djibouti to Ethiopia, and that the UNHCR urgently explore ways in which refugees and refugee organizations can be directly involved in the planning, implementation and monitoring of future voluntary repatriation programmes.

7. *Resettlement*

Africa prefers to solve refugee problems within the African context. However, it is recognized that there are special cases where resettlement is the most suitable durable solution. The Symposium recommends:
7.1 That refugee resettlement be the subject of a special study, which examines the opportunities for the resettlement of African refugees in areas other than North America and Western Europe.
7.2 That when this study is completed, the UNHCR, NGOs, relevant governments and refugee representatives meet to discuss its recommendations, make proposals for action, and implement these proposals.

7.3 That in view of the fact that resettlement often deprives refugee communities of their most skilled and talented members, relevant organizations and refugee representatives consider methods of reducing the demand for resettlement where it is not essential to the health and safety of the refugees concerned.

7.4 That resettlement countries examine their current selection procedures and consider granting priority to:

(i) vulnerable refugees, especially the handicapped;

(ii) refugees who have failed to gain recognition from the host government;

(iii) refugees who have been granted mandated status;

(iv) refugees with or without the recognition of the host government and whose protection cannot be guaranteed in the host country;

(v) refugees whose skills are not required in their country of first asylum and whose prospects of returning to their country of origin are remote.

7.5 That selection for resettlement always be determined on the basis of real need, and not on the basis of special connections or any other form of discrimination, and that, except in special protection cases, the host government also be involved in ensuring fair selection according to the priorities cited above.

7.6 That, where possible, resettlement be carried out on a family basis.

8. UNHCR/Host Government/NGO Relations

The Symposium recommends:

8.1 That all refugees be provided with full and accurate information regarding their own rights and the obligations of the host government, the UNHCR and relevant NGOs.

8.2 That all refugees be provided with full and accurate information regarding the roles of the relationship between the host government, the UNHCR and relevant NGOs.

8.3 That the UNHCR consider expanding the brief of its Public Information Officers to include information for refugees, and provide funding for the publication of that information.

8.4 That the UNHCR finance the production of 'Blue Books' by refugees for refugees.

8.5 That the UNHCR guarantee all refugees access to a regular postal service.

8.6 That refugees be provided with regular, full and accurate information regarding any events in their settlement area, in the host country generally, in their country of origin or elsewhere that is relevant to their situation.

8.7 That refugee representatives, however chosen, receive orientation and training that will enable them to perform their duties in an effective and efficient manner.

8.8 That, in drawing up projects for UNHCR funding, governmental and non-governmental agencies include information on the nature of refugee participation in the planning, implementation, monitoring and evaluation of the project, and that funding be withheld from proposed projects which fail to include such information.

8.9 That refugee organizations engaged in humanitarian work be given NGO status in the country or countries in which they are operational.

8.10 That NGOs refrain from withdrawing from projects before their planned completion dates, and that NGOs work through and with local staff, refugees and refugee organizations, thereby allowing projects to continue after the withdrawal of the NGO.

8.11 That independent research into refugee issues be encouraged by the UNHCR, NGOs and host governments, and that funding and other forms of support be provided for the establishment of specialized centres dedicated to refugee research and the training of refugee workers.

States Party to UN and OAU Convention

African states which are party to the 1951 UN Convention and/or the 1967 Protocol relating to the Status of Refugees:

Algeria	Gabon	Rwanda
Angola	Gambia	Sao Tomé & Principé
Benin	Ghana	Senegal
Botswana	Guinea	Seychelles
Burkina Faso	Guinea-Bissau	Sierra Leone
Burundi	Kenya	Somalia

Cameroon	Lesotho	Sudan
Cape-Verde (P)	Liberia	Swaziland (P)
Central African Rep.	Madagascar (C)	Togo
Chad	Mali	Tunisia
Congo	Mauritania	Uganda
Ivory Coast	Morocco	Tanzania
Djibouti	Mozambique (C)	Zaire
Egypt	Niger	Zambia
Equatorial Guinea	Nigeria	Zimbabwe
Ethiopia		

(C) Party to the 1951 Convention only
(P) Party to the 1967 Protocol only

List of states not party to the OAU Convention of 1979 governing the specific aspects of refugee problems in Africa (January 1987):

Botswana
Cape Verde
Djibouti
Guinea
Guinea Bissau
Ivory Coast
Kenya
Lesotho
Madagascar
Malawi
Mauritius
Mozambique
Sao Tomé and Principé
Sierra Leone
Swaziland
Uganda

6 Women: The Gender Factor in the African Social Situation

Filomina Chioma Steady

The Dependency Crisis and African Women

In the aftermath of the United Nations Decade for Women and eight years into the International Development Strategy for the Third United Nations Development Decade, the social and economic conditions of the majority of African women have not improved and may, in fact, have worsened. The international record is replete with strategies at the national, regional and international level, that for the majority of African women will never be implemented.

The current crisis of development is a crisis of dependency that has been systematically maintained by a combination of unjust and racist international economic relations and the continuing synergistic alliance between the economic elites of Europe and North America and the influential elites of Africa. These factors have been aggravated by natural disasters and life-threatening epidemics affecting several regions of the continent.

African women, historically and in modern times, have experienced many structural disadvantages by virtue of their gender, reproductive and productive roles and the nature of their integration into the world economy. African women also, historically and in modern times, have made significant contributions to the positive development of their societies and in promoting the well-being and welfare of their families and households and communities.

For the majority of Africans, particularly women, the articulation between African economic systems and the northern economic superstructure has resulted in 'regressive development'. 'Regressive development' is the process of economic deterioration of the majority of African nations and the worsening of the condition of the majority of African peoples brought about by intractable and inimical states of dependency. Within the context of dependency, African nations serve as hosts to northern parasitical nations whose primary interest in Africa is to maintain the status quo, which ensures their economic well-being and prosperity. Development for Africa is, therefore, hardly possible within the context of dependency.

Protracted recession, the lowering of prices for primary products and large-scale unemployment have been exacerbated by the conditions imposed by the International Monetary Fund. Its structural adjustment policies include removal of government subsidies for staple foods and fuel, retrenchment in public enterprises, increase in export crop production and devaluation of local currencies. These conditions result in untold human misery and a crisis of survival for poor people who constitute the majority of the African population. There is an increasing and intensified trend towards the pauperization of large numbers of African people, particularly women in both rural and urban areas.

Women's positions, as major actors ensuring the mainstay of most subsistence economies, are being eroded as many African countries are plunged into protracted states of economic chaos. Several remedial policies proposed by international financial institutions have in fact become more oppressing than the problems they claim to resolve so that it can be rightly said that structural adjustment policies of the International Monetary Fund are becoming tantamount to genocide in many African countries.

The twin processes of 'development' and 'underdevelopment' have been convincingly presented by many scholars as interdependent aspects of the expansion of western capitalism in the nineteenth century. This interdependent framework has remained virtually unchanged throughout the colonial, post-colonial and modern periods. It represents a process that conforms to retrogressive development and has been well articulated by dependency theorists as:

> a situation in which the economy of certain countries is conditioned by the development and expansion of another economy to which the former is subjected. The relation of interdependence between two or more economies and between these and world trade, assumes the form of dependence when some countries (the dominant ones) can expand and can be self-sustaining while other countries (the dependent ones) can do this only as a reflection of that expansion. (Dos Santos, 1968)

The present economic crisis and structural adjustment policies have become the best empirical evidence of the validity of dependency theory. For Africa the work of Samir Amin is exemplary of this theoretical position (Amin, 1974).

With regard to issues of gender, women generally occupy subordinate roles in the division of labour at the international and national levels. Consquently, retrogressive development results in the subordination and oppression of the majority of women and in the worsening of their socio-economic conditions, irrespective of their increasing participation and integration into so-called development.

The dominant model of development promotes the priorities and interests of the elites of the economically dominant nations of the northern hemisphere at the expense of the socio-economic and welfare needs of the populations of the south. As a result special groups in society, who have been marginalized on the basis of gender, age, race and class, have either remained outside of the development process or become integrated in exploitative ways.

Historically, African women have been differentially integrated into the world economic system, serving primarily as a labour reserve and a mainstay for the subsistence and reproductive sectors. Women's subsistence activities in Africa as in other regions of the developing world have been incorporated into the market economy in a *subsidizing role* in order to maintain the low wages paid to men. As has been noted by several scholars, endless hours of unpaid labour performed by women to physically sustain themselves, their children and their husbands have been necessary to ensure the extraction of huge profits by foreign-owned industries and companies throughout Africa.

Because of the predominance of women in domestic activities and the unequal and transitory way in which they have been incorporated into the labour force, they remain essentially 'outside' of modern productive processes. As a result they are marginalized and disenfranchised in terms of political participation, decision-making, and autonomy. They have become the ultimate victims of retrogressive development.

Retrogressive development has resulted in a situation of reliance on food imports that imposes severe strains on a country's foreign exchange earnings and undermines a country's ability to feed itself. In situations where there is an additional hardship indebtedness, this can result in grave social consequences. As a result of northern-inspired policies that stress export crop production to ensure 'comparative advantage', many countries in Africa continue to emphasize the production of export crops and are increasingly relying on food imports and food aid. These policies were instigated by countries of the north during the first and second UN Development decades and favoured the large commercial grain producers of the United States, Canada and Australia. By reinforcing the production processes initiated through colonialism, these policies perpetuate retrogressive development and undermine the food production activities of women.

Within this context of development, even countries that have been able to achieve self-sufficiency in food production cannot always ensure that there is equitable distribution to all people as long as the model of development creates and reinforces inequality and prevents access of poor people to adequate and nutritious food supply. Inequalities in distribution can create similar or worse crises than actual food shortages, with even more severe social human consequences for special groups such as women, children and the aged.

According to a recent report of the Food and Agricultural Organization (FAO, 1988) food staples are expected to fall to the lowest level in more than a decade world-wide, indicating that Africa's food problems are far from being over. World cereal production, particularly of rice and wheat, would need to increase in 1988 by at least 6 per cent or over 100m tons. The report also noted that cereal import demand in 1987/88 has risen following poor harvests in a number of importing countries while a number of low-income food-deficit developing countries continue to face emergencies and require food assistance. Particular attention was given to the precarious situation in several African countries, in particular Ethiopia, Sudan, Mozambique, Zimbabwe and several Sahelian countries. Even for countries not yet directly affected, such as Kenya, Botswana, Sierra Leone and Ghana, since about 40 per cent of the rural households in these countries are headed by women (UN, 1985) the threat posed by food scarcity would probably be exacerbated for these households because of the generally low economic situation of the majority of rural women.

In many areas of Africa, particularly the Sahelian region, the food crisis is closely related to the fuel crisis, since wood and other vegetable residues provide the bulk of the energy needs for people in rural areas. As a result, deforestation, loss of soil fertility, low human power productivity and poor standard of living have been the characteristic features of these areas.

Perhaps the most devastating effects of the present economic crisis is the destruction of the subsistence economic base in which women play a central role. Some of this destruction pertains to natural disasters such as drought and desertification but most are a result of inimical development processes propelled by world economic pressures that are threatening the viability of many African countries and destroying the environment. According to a UNEP report 'Africa...is suffering from continued drain on, and degradation of, its natural resources - plant-cover, soils, water, animal resources and climate. . . .The general degradation has led to the poverty of African people and the lowering of their quality of life' (UNEP, 1985). Development problems such as chronic unemployment, illiteracy, inadequate sanitation, prevalent disease and malnutrition, which has been viewed as temporary, are now endemic to the African social reality. The gravity of the African crisis is underscored by the fact that women, especially the poor who constitute the majority, are now likely to become even more marginalized and disenfranchised instead of becoming the focus of all development efforts. Women's role in subsistence economics is not only pivotal, as has been widely recognized, but critical. In agriculture, forestry and fisheries the role of women in ensuring food sufficiency for their families and communities cannot be overstated. One study has noted that since the food-water-fuel crises are interlinked, and local people are to be the backbone of development efforts and their resolution, women - especially those who are poor and landless - must be explicitly recognized as key human elements in the linkages and as active agents in any resolution (Sen and Crown, 1987).

Gender, Science, Technology in the Context of Dependency

Another poignant aspect of retrogressive development relates to science and technology and its effects on women

(Steady, 1987). The crisis in development is related in part to the ideology and the macro-historical environment that have shaped the development of science and technology in the west and the mode of its transfer to developing countries. Science and technology developed along hierarchical and exclusionary lines and have been controlled for more than 300 years by the elites of western society. Through colonialism the transfer of technology to the south involved the transfer of western structures and ideological underpinnings without regard for indigenous scientific and technological alternatives and traditions.

Consequently, science and technology have created and reinforced inequality on the basis of race, class and gender. Most scientific and technological institutions are based in urban areas where colonial infrastructures and facilities for the most part remain intact. Most urban areas in Africa were designed to facilitate the colonial exploitation of Africa's resources and continue to function in that capacity today.

Gender differences have always been determining factors in the transfer of technology since most scientific and technologically based activities in Africa have been geared towards the extraction of minerals and cash crops for export. These activities, including capital intensive industrialization, are more directly vital to ensuring extraction of resources and usually represent the economic domain in which men are predominant.

In addition, research, scientific engineering and technological improvements have been made in the male dominated spheres of production. The priority given to cash crop production, a vital aspect of colonial exploitation, continues to be emphasized by the international financial institutions in spite of its detrimental effects on food production, which is usually in the domain of female economic activities. According to the FAO, rural women working on small-scale farms now produce 90 per cent of the locally consumed food.

The modernization of agriculture through the use of high technology further exploits the Third World countries, particularly those in Africa, since this type of agriculture is heavily dependent on inputs manufactured in profit-making multinational corporations with wide-ranging monopolies in their production.

Within the current socio-economic framework of a development crisis, women in Third World countries, particularly African women, have also become victims of scientific and technological engineering in several ways. Some of these relate to their *labour* and some relate specifically to their *biology* (ibid.).

The documentation on the process of incorporation of Third World women as cheap sources of labour within the framework of the international division of labour is extensive. Although more widespread in Asia and Latin America whereas many as 92-95 per cent of the labour force in export-oriented electronics, textiles, agricultural and food processing industries is female, there is evidence of a trend towards similar patterns being developed in Africa as conditions necessitate relocation of these industries in order to further increase profit margins. In countries such as Swaziland and Ivory Coast (McFadden, 1982; Traove, 1982), where transnational companies have established agro-industries, there is evidence of the recurrence of the pattern of exploitation characteristic of export processing zones in Asia and Latin America.

With regard to the exploitation of the female body, African women have been routinely used in experimentation with dangerous drugs. Through technology transfer, the African female biological system has become subjected to the use of unsafe fertility regulating drugs such as Depo-Provera. In the absence of genuine informed consent many African women have also become victims of involuntary sterilization, a practice that has been widely used on black women, native American women and Hispanic women in the United States. New developments in AIDS research, biotechnology and genetic engineering would no doubt also create new opportunities for the unethical use of African women in experimentation unless vigilant efforts are made to prevent these trends.

As the following statement illustrates and predicts, imported science and technology have served in some measure to maintain the hegemony and control of the north, resulting in exploitation, unethical practices and economic and social crises that are unprecedented in modern times.

> Science and technology have emerged as primary instruments of power and social control, with the major industrialized countries, especially the superpowers, relying more on science and technology as a means of maintaining their dominance in that system. Notwithstanding beachheads of technological competence and scientific excellence in the Third World the technological gap between the North and the South has widened during this period because of the near monopoly that a few industrialized countries have acquired on the generation and productive use of the technology based on modern science. Development strategies relying on importation of capital-intensive socially inappropriate, environmentally destructive Western technology cannot but lead to a massive global equity crisis in the 1980's. (Moorehouse, 1979)

The process inherent in the transfer of western science and technology to the Third World has been described as 'structural and cultural aggression', since the demand created by the implantation of western technology for spare parts, knowledge, skills and new technologies enables the dominant countries to maintain their command position (D'Onofrio-Flores, 1982).

The debt crisis represents the most devastating aspects of retrogressive development and according to one study can threaten the collapse of the world financial system because huge amounts of capital are flowing from poor to rich nations in debt servicing. The net transfer of capital from the poor nations to the rich nations increased from $7 billion in 1981 to $73 billion in 1985. In 1985, new borrowing and rescheduling was $41 billion, but debt servicing was much higher at $114 billion (Clairmont and Cavagagh, 1987).

According to the IMF there has been a major increase in the total debt from $500 billion in 1980 to $800 billion in 1985. Latin America's debt burden totals $368 billion (46 per cent); Asia's total is $304 billion (38 per cent); and Africa's total is $129 billion (16 per cent). Although Africa's debt is only about 16 per cent of the total, the burden of debt servicing is greater because of its weaker economies and their weaker gross domestic production (ibid.). This is aggravated by the dependency on primary products that are subject to the fluctuation of international markets.

The decline in commodity prices has meant that more commodities are needed to be sold at lower prices in return for more expensive imported goods and services as well as foreign exchange needed for the endless expansion of interests and amortization payments on debts (ibid.). The underdevelopment of Africa as the result of the development of Europe and North America has moved to an even more ominous stage in modern times.

In response to the debt crisis women's employment in export agriculture is likely to grow in some countries particularly in agribusiness plantations and estates. However, this type of employment is usually as exploitative as the export-oriented industrialization prevalent in export-processing zones because of its temporary and unprotective nature (Sen and Crown, 1987).

Even more tragic is the fact that the strain imposed by the debt would affect women in more fundamental ways. Women often constitute the majority among the poor and are frequently responsible for the care and well-being of the dependent members of societies such as children, the aged, the disabled and the sick.

Another dimension of the debt burden pertains to the fact that the consequent instability of the international monetary and financial system not only makes it difficult to service the debts in the short term, but makes long-term planning almost impossible (ibid.). Debt repudiation, which will by no means end Africa's problems, but go a long way to resolving some of them is now inevitable and can in fact be regarded as long overdue.

> It is impossible that the outstanding principal of Third World debt will ever be repaid. Simply deferring interest payments and principal to the transnational banking circuit and seeking for rescheduling agreements would perhaps mitigate the bleeding and the pain. It can by no means stop the hemorrhage. In fact neither can the principal nor the interest ever be repaid. Nor is it desirable that the debt (interest and principal) be repaid. Debt repudiation stands out as the rational solutions for the Third World. (Clairmont and Cavagagh, 1987)

Beyond the Decade

The United Nations Decade for Women has served in some measure to mediate the contradiction inherent in the world economic system that promotes 'retrogressive development'. The structural disadvantages experienced by women in most countries were seen as requiring multilateral action. The Decade was therefore established 'to transform fundamental relationships within society to ensure a system which excludes the possibility of exploitation'.

Throughout the Decade, the various International Women's Conferences have addressed the issue of exploitation on various levels, starting with the main focus on gender equality at the International Women's Year conference in Mexico, which produced the World Plan of Action in 1975. Subsequent conferences examined the linkages between gender and inequality and inequalities between and within nations. In this regard the Copenhagen World Conference of 1980 that produced the Programme of Action addressed the problem of unjust international economic relations between poor and rich countries. In particular it viewed the history of colonialism, imperialism and neo-colonialism as root causes of women's inequality and oppression in Third World countries.

This link was further elaborated at the Nairobi Conference of 1985, which in addition to the other levels of inequality also addressed the issue of inequalities *among* women. Consequently the *Nairobi Forward-Looking Strategies* established guidelines and priorities for underprivileged and vulnerable groups of women as well as for women in situations of armed conflict; women subject to oppressive and imperialistic regimes; women under apartheid in South Africa and Namibia and women oppressed by foreign occupation.

At the Nairobi Conference it became clear that global processes that reinforce the subordination of women and perpetuate oppressive regimes were on the increase and result from a number of factors that include the worsening world economic crisis, increasing global tensions, environmental degradation, and the persistence of the retrogressive model of development, which among other things perpetuates unequal power relations between men and women. After Nairobi, women's issues could no longer be isolated, since they affected political, economic, social and cultural spheres of society. Women's issues became finally accepted as life issues and consequently as political issues. Nonetheless, the framework for the implementation of strategies remain for the most part reformist.

Equality

The majority of countries in Africa have, over the Decade, established guidelines and specific plans for the advancement of women in national development plans and policies and recognize the need for special efforts to be made to address the critical needs of poorer and more vulnerable women. Many countries have given priority to all the relevant issues such as ensuring basic needs and the full beneficial participation of women in the development process. Several measures to increase women's productive roles, which include establishing income-generation projects, strengthening and supporting the informal sector and facilitating access of rural women to resources, have been included. In the area of human resource development, health and educational policies have included improving the status of women in terms of literacy, education, technical and vocational training, access to primary health care, nutritional and family planning services. Commitment to policy is, however, not a guarantee of implementation and without adequate budgetary allocations these policy guidelines remain symbolic rather than instrumental.

One of the major instruments of the Decade for the Advancement of Women has been the establishment of national machineries. These are interdisciplinary and multisectoral institutions within the government establishment for the purpose of accelerating the achievement of equal opportunities for women and their full integration into national life.

> Where it does not exist, national machinery preferably at the highest level of government, where appropriate, should be established. By national machinery should be understood, not only the establishment of central institutions at the national level, but furthermore, where appropriate, the establishment of a comprehensive network of extensions in the form of commissions, offices or posts at different levels, including the local administrative level because of its better capacity of dealing with specific local situations, as well as working units in the relevant branches of administration, in order to ensure the effective implementation of action programmes ensuring the equality of men and women. (Copenhagen, 1980)

A number of countries in Africa have established some form of institutional structure within the government that has responsibility for women's issues. Many of these institutions, with few exceptions, are not very effective, operate under serious resource constraints and often lack the support of the executive branch of government. In general, institutions that are located in the office of the chief executive may have a better chance to be truly effective and to have greater access to resources.

Some progress has been made in promoting equality between the sexes in many countries through legislative measures to end discriminative practices against women. One major international instrument that provided the framework and stimulus for most legislative changes relating to sex discrimination was the Convention on the Elimination of all Forms of Discrimination against Women, which came into force in 1980. It contains measures to eliminate discrimination against women in such areas as political and public life, education, employment, marriage and the family and ensures women the right to nationality. It also seeks to protect the rights of rural women and gives special attention to the suppression of prostitution and the elimination of stereotyped views that promote a negative image of women. The convention has been signed by 96 states of which 30 are in Africa and ratified by 76, 18 of which are in Africa.

Despite the significant progress that has been made in the field of legislation in many countries, *de facto* discrimination still persists and several countries that have ratified the convention make reservations on several articles thereby weakening it.

Many of the legal constraints on equality can be attributed to the persistence of stereotypes and attitudes prescribing restricted roles for women and encouraging sex discrimination. Customary and scriptural law can enhance women's position in some instances, but may also prove detrimental to women because of the outmoded nature of many of their codes and prescriptions. In some situations where they are in conflict with statutory law particularly on matters relating to inheritance and marriage, customary law can be manipulated to women's disadvantage. To give one example, because of the influence of customary rules on matters of paternity, the nationality of children continues to favour the father in several African countries where there are patrilineal rules of descent. Furthermore, women's mobility can be circumscribed by customary law. In some countries such as Benin, Gabon, Ivory Coast and Zaire married women could move only with the consent of their husbands (UN, 1985).

Discriminatory practices are still inherent in a number of civil and administrative codes so that there is further need to strengthen the legal capacity of women in relation to ensuring access to services and facilities.

With regard to the issue of violence against women several countries now have legislative provisions preventing the abuse of women and children since this has been recognized as a world-wide problem. Nevertheless, there is a great need for concerted and comprehensive action to protect the victims, restrain and punish the culprits and ensure long-term prevention. A recent expert group meeting on violence in the family held in Vienna, Austria, identified as a root cause of the abuse of women the subordinate position of women, which results from the unequal power relations between men and women.

The real constraints on legal equality for women relates to inequalities engendered in other spheres through the process of development. In light of this, poor women will be limited by the constraints imposed by economic forces that limit access to legal services and information. With the exception of the more educated and fortunate members of society who are aware of their legal rights, have resources to retain legal counsel and have developed some degree of familiarity with legal processes and procedures, most women have no legal recourse, financial backing, or awareness of their rights.

Development Trends

Women's indispensable role in development was best expressed by President Julius Nyerere when he said: 'National development is dependent upon the women of Africa and cannot take place without them. A person does not walk very far or very fast on one leg. How can we expect half the people to be able to develop the nation?' (ECA, 1985).

It is now well recognized that women must constitute an integral part of any strategy to develop the political, economic, social and cultural aspects of life and must be ensured an equal distribution of the benefits. According to the United Nations Decade for Women development should be total and embrace all spheres of life as a means to furthering equality between the sexes and promoting the maintenance of peace. In order to ensure women's full participation in development, it was also considered necessary to increase women's autonomy so that they can achieve equal partnership with men and realize their own strengths, talents and potentials. Measures outlined in the International Development Strategy of the Third United Nations Development Decade were seen as important for improving the status of women, particularly if they were to be fully implemented within the framework of a New International Economic Order.

These were words of optimism as women mobilized around their faith in multilateralism as an instrument to ensure women's advancement and improve the human condition. The period of the Decade and beyond have, however, not fulfilled these hopes. The Decade began with much promise for economic growth and prosperity, but by the beginning of the 1980s this optimism gave way to pessimism as the world economy stagnated or plummeted into a downward spiral. As one development decade gave way to another, the problems of poverty, illiteracy and malnutrition increased. Added to these problems were inflation, the debt crisis, protectionism, large-scale unemployment and world recession. Within the context of dependency the economic recovery of a number of countries of the northern hemisphere was secured at the expense of countries of the south, which further worsened their position.

Economic factors sustaining recession and a shrinking of resources are increasingly emerging as formidable obstacles to the advancement of African women. By virtue of their lower status in society women are disproportionately affected by negative trends in development and are often the worst victims of poverty. The outcome is an increasing paradox between the international commitment to the advancement of women and the increasing structural imbalance in the global economy. Contradictions between the reality of economic recession in most developing countries and the policies and programmes for integrating women into development present a picture that on the one hand shows expansion in expectations and on the other contraction in resources.

The net result is that women, particularly disadvantaged women, become even further marginalized. Given the current economic conditions in most developing countries, the price-tag for achieving the goals and objectives of the Decade for Women, namely equality, development and peace, appears high. It competes with resources for combatting poverty, malnutrition and endemic diseases as well as expenditures for defence. However, the neglect of women will be even more costly in the end since this would not only represent wastage of valuable human resources but tragic short-sightedness in failing to recognize that the creative involvement of women offers the only hope of a viable solution to Africa's current crisis.

Peace

The absence of peace in many parts of the world has been viewed as one of the major obstacles to the advancement of women. Peace is closely related to equality and development and affects all nations and regions as well as the whole international community as a human entity. Although global war has been avoided, several areas of the world have witnessed at least one major international conflict. Women's lives are affected by wars and their participation in peace efforts is increasingly becoming critical.

Despite the policy proclamations and commitments of the international community to national and international programmes of action for the advancement of women, other issues are given priority in the execution of budgets. The budget for many African countries shows more being spent on defence than on health and education, the major sectors that enhance social development by developing human resources. In Africa generally, spending on the military, arms imports and the armed forces exceeds health and education budgets by 4-5% (Sivard, 1985). Furthermore, reactions to the negative consequences of structural adjustment in the form of civil disobedience, strikes and political instability have led to an increasing need for arms to control popular revolts. A well-known and sinister dimension to retrogressivedevelopment is that more military expenditures are being increasingly used for suppressing *internal* revolts and popular uprising than for purposes of defence from external aggression.

The advance in technology has emphasized the manufacture and proliferation of deadly weapons in the whole biosphere and even into space. One important aspect of this technological revolution is the capacity for destruction over large areas. A lucrative arms trade has developed as a result. Although estimates of the overall value of the international flow of arms are not very reliable, in the 20 years ending in 1983, eight countries accounted for 85 per cent of $305 billion in world arms exports. The two superpowers alone had two-thirds of the export trade. The largest market for arms was in the developing countries. Over the 20-year period they imported military equipment to a total value of $223 billion, equivalent to about three-quarters of all arms imports and more than one-half of the economic development aid expended by industrialized countries (ibid.). As Perez de Cuellar, Secretary General of the United Nations, put it in 1984, 'The arms trade impoverishes the receiver and debases the supplier. There is a striking resemblance to the drug trade' (ibid.).

Apartheid represents the most important peace issue in Africa. The continuation of apartheid threatens the peace and security of the continent and has had devastating effects on women in South Africa and Namibia. This is now only too well known. Also well known are the heroic struggles of African women against the diabolical system of apartheid. It represents the most extreme form of retrogressive development and structural violence upheld by constitutional injustice and is strengthened by the alliance of major so-called 'democratic nations'. The security and well-being of the Front Line States is constantly threatened by the political, military and economic aggressiveness of the apartheid regime of South Africa. Women and children in these states are greatly affected by these realities as are a large number of African women from South Africa and Namibia who have become refugees as a result of apartheid. The destruction of apartheid, which is the epitome of social decadence, is a necessary precondition for the true liberation of the continent from political, economic, social and cultural domination.

Employment

Women's participation in the labour force world-wide is increasing, but conditions of work as well as salary and wage levels remain inadequate. According to the estimates and projections of the International Labour Office, women's participation in the labour force stands at about 35 per cent. This has been increasing since 1950 and the trend is expected to continue so that by the year 2000 the global female labour force will be 900 million.

Judging from the available data world-wide, women are presently more than one-fourth of the industrial labour force and almost two-fifths of the agricultural labour force and services. Regional variations are significant. In Africa and South Asia, male labour force participation rates will increase at the same rate as women up to the year 2000. In all of the other regions, and especially in northern Europe and North America, female participation rates will increase faster than males (UN, 1986).

Although employment opportunities are increasing for women world-wide the majority continue to be employed at the lower levels of the labour force hierarchy and to experience discrimination, low levels of pay, minimum or no insurance or maternity benefits and sexual harassment. Persistent sex discrimination often results in inadequate education and training, limited career opportunities and restricted mobility in the number of occupations. In addition, women often experience institutional and cultural constraints in terms of participation at the decision-making and management levels of most occupations. Women's domestic responsibilities also impose constraints on employment that have not been adequately resolved in a large number of countries. Although a number of measures have been endorsed to promote equality in the labour market in terms of wages, training, compensations, promotion, expansion of employment and income procurement opportunities for women, these have not often been accompanied by provision of social services to support working mothers, nor the sharing of domestic responsibilities with men, nor the establishment of shorter and more flexible working hours for all. One study conducted in Tanzania has shown that, in addition to child care that goes on throughout the day, rural women spend an average of 70 hours a week on domestic tasks involving cooking, collecting firewood, fetching water and pounding grain (Ngalwa, 1974).

For a few African women in countries such as Botswana

and Mauritius participation in the labour force has been substantial in the professions and in the technical fields but for most African women formal employment is primarily concentrated in the semi-skilled and unskilled jobs in the manufacturing and service sectors. Trends in labour force participation in other regions include job crowding, sex segregation, wage differentials, limited opportunities for training and mobility, and minimim or no participation in trade unions.

For the majority of African women employment opportunities are severely limited as a result of the chronic and generally high unemployment in many African countries. According to estimates women constitute only 10-15 per cent of the African formal labour market. Consequently, women's economic activities have been concentrated primarily in the informal labour market. Female activity rates in this sector are as high as 90 per cent in some countries in West Africa, according to ILO estimates. Despite declarations and strategies, priority has not been given to improving conditions in the informal labour market, to ensure credit facilities, training, as well as insurance benefits and compensations for women in this sector. The recognition and valuation of this sector is important because of women's economic contribution in this vital economic sphere, which includes agriculture, food processing, trade, services, home industries, health care, etc.

According to ILO estimates and projections more than half of the world's working women are in agriculture, many of them in Africa. The World Survey on the Role of Women in Development estimated that women constitute almost half of the agricultural labour force in many countries in Africa and more than half in countries such as Botswana, Cameroon and Sierra Leone.

In view of the key role played by women as food producers in many regions of the world and their subsequent economic contributions to society, several endorsed measures need to be implemented to integrate them fully in all aspects of the planning, implementation, monitoring and evaluation of all agricultural development and food security programmes. In addition, emphasis has to be placed on their equal participation in agricultural training, technological research, access to agricultural inputs, credits and social services. Women's participation in the construction, management and maintenance of irrigation and water conservation systems as workers is essential if the crisis in food production is to be averted.

Data from countries of both the northern and southern hemispheres shows that, despite women's increasing participation in the labour force, they tend to be concentrated in specific jobs in the tertiary sector. For Third World countries where much of this type of employment is a result of the expansion of urbanization rather than industrialization, female employment has been predominantly in the lower echelons of the services sector, and for some countries primarily in domestic service and prostitution. As in the case of Brazil, 'The growth of occupations such as domestic service confirms once again that capitalist development does not always improve women's position in the wage labour market, especially that of lower class' (Vasques de Miranda).

The beneficial effect of tourism in Africa remains highly questionable when one considers its effects on female employment. The emphasis on tourism in some African countries has increased the incidence of prostitution, even though tourism is of very little economic benefit to most countries. With the possible exception of countries such as Kenya, South Africa and the Maghreb region, revenue from tourism is generally low and investment high. Apart from 'subsidizing' European leisure by providing a cheap source of male and female labour, tourism often creates an unconsious 'colour bar' through the segregation of tourist facilities and establishments. With regard to prostitution, the resulting high rates of this activity are often accompanied by negative medical and social consequences, the promotion of an alien pattern of consumption, and worsening of the rate of inflation. Even more ominous is the fact that a substantial number of tourist industries are operated and controlled from European and North American capitals where most of the profits are expropriated (Steady, 1982).

As is well known, a large percentage of construction material for buildings, equipment, furniture and other goods used in tourist facilities, as well as food and beverages and other consumer items are imported from overseas (Da Gama Santos, 1985). The emphasis on tourism in some countries is a reflection of the dependency syndrome, which promotes an external orientation to development and the deteriorating economic condition of large segments of the population. If for the woman from a poor background, prostitution, particularly within the context of tourism, is the only alternative to destitution, then something is seriously wrong with the development process. In the interest of promoting beneficial development it is important to analyse the alternatives to tourism in countries where it is counterproductive and cost ineffective. Emphasis on agriculture and manufacturing, if well planned and executed, could have a more beneficial impact on the economy in terms of providing jobs, developing rural communities, reducing dependency and promoting a sense of national pride. At the very least tourism should be part of a comprehensive development programme and not exist solely to promote European or North American economic interests. According to one study:

The most underdeveloped societies and simultaneously highly dependent on tourism appear to show high negative socio-economic effects such as large foreign exchange leakages and imports of goods to meet tourism investment and operational requirements, high capital intensity of this industry resulting in high capital/labor relations, low impact on regional development, low degree of leakage effects on the economy, adverse effects on agricultural development and socio-economic and cultural disruption of local communities. (Ibid.)

Health

The importance of health in promoting human resource development and enhancing women's productivity and well-being cannot be overemphasized. In reviewing the health status of women, life expectancy rates increased significantly in the developing countries during the UN Decade for Women so that in 1985, for example the average girl could expect to live 18 years longer than her mother. Yet in most of the developing world, particularly in sub-Saharan Africa and South Asia, the life expectancy for the average woman is still low, falling below 50 years. The quality of life has also dropped significantly for the majority of African women.

Although the Decade has facilitated the implementation of measures to promote women's health, much still remains to be done, since problems of chronic ill health are linked to retrogressive development. Women in developing countries, particularly in Africa, face special health needs that are sometimes influenced by environmental and economic factors. Poverty, hard manual work, endemic diseases, inadequate public health facilities and poor nutrition all have detrimental effects on women's health. Some cultural practices such as female circumcision have also been proven to be injurious to women's health.

The AIDS epidemic now poses serious threats to African women in some countries because of the heterosexual nature of its spread, some of which can be attributed to tourism. Many European and North American tour enterprises promote exotic sex tourism with racial overtones. Sex tourism must account for a substantial amount of the spread of AIDS in Africa even though this has not been given much prominence in the media. Indeed, consistent with the racist mentality, Africa was instead once blamed as the continent where AIDS originated.

In general, women's health needs are often ignored by health planners, and their roles as the most important providers of health care and health education are also often ignored. The World Health Organization's global strategy of health for all by the year 2000 places great importance on the participation of women and has established effective indicators for monitoring women's health.

One of the most essential elements of primary health care determined by WHO is maternal and child health care that includes skilled help in childbirth. A number of training programmes have been initiated in African countries for training of traditional birth attendants and for upgrading the skills of the medical and paramedical personnel working in the area of maternal and child care. In the developing countries, an estimated 50 per cent of births are assisted only by traditional birth attendants or female relatives, and in Africa the proportion is close to 75 per cent.

In devising plans for the future it will be important to promote participation of women from the grass-roots level in primary health care programmes and to stress community health care schemes while promoting preventive health measures supported by an adequate health care infrastructure. Activities such as tourism should be discouraged when they become a health menace to the African people.

The International Conference on Population held in Mexico City in 1984 stressed the link between the status of women and population issues and the importance of women's participation in the planning, implementation, monitoring and evaluation of population policies. The advancement of women will be influenced by the ability of women to determine their family size, the determination of society to provide support services for working women, and the willingness of men to share in household responsibilities. Women's role in reproduction and domestic duties continues to be disproportionately high and requires the support of governments, non-governmental organizations and men in order to facilitate women's equal participation in production and in the public sphere. Traditionally, there has been a tendency to *disinvest* in women's resource development. This needs to change so that women can develop their full potential. Without doubt the link between population and development is particularly relevant to women.

Education

Health and employment are closely linked to education, which for African women presents some contradictions. On the positive side the gender gap is narrowing in terms of basic education. Vocational education for girls as well as schemes to train girls in new fields involving technical education have increased. In some instances efforts have been made to review educational materials, school books and literature in order to revise the stereotyped images and roles usually portrayed of women. Despite these gains, the number of boys in education still outnumber girls in the majority of countries and the education of boys is still given priority. Furthermore, the dropout rate for girls is still higher than for boys. According to UNESCO's estimates and projections girls' education quadrupled between 1950 and 1985. Despite these increases, 25 per cent of children of primary-school age do not attend school. A large percentage of these are girls and in Africa the rate is even higher, particularly in rural areas. Boys outnumber girls at both primary and secondary levels of education, and the differences become even more marked at the higher levels. In the developing countries in particular there are almost two men to every woman at university level.

Illiteracy continues to be widespread in the developing countries, particularly in Africa, even though some progress has been made. It is more marked among women and has been correlated to poverty. At least 60 per cent of the 500 million women who are unable to read and write live in countries where the average per caput income in 1980 was below $300 and where education is not free. In many of these African countries, 80 per cent of women over the age of 25 have never received any schooling at all.

Although some progress has been made in the technical

and vocational fields, these are often confined to domestic science-type subjects and textbooks are still replete with images of women in passive and traditional roles.

Several constraints continue to exist for women in terms of *access* to education, particularly in the attainment of higher education. These are bolstered by cultural stereotypes about women's domestic destiny and the supplementary nature of their earnings despite the fact that an increasingly large number of households are being headed by women. In many societies girls are expected to help with domestic chores that can divert both time and energy from school work. Teenage pregnancy often acts as a deterrent to educational attainment and advancement of girls, since this invariably results in withdrawal from school.

Numerous strategies have been adopted that seek to expand the enrolment of girls at all levels of education and in all fields, particularly in science and technology as well as to increase vocational opportunities and eradicate illiteracy. However, progress continues to be very slow and has regressed in some instances. Any serious action to rectify this must give preferential treatment to girls and make concerted efforts to eliminate cultural stereotypes restricting female education. Above all the structural links that promote and sustain the development of African countries within the context of dependency will have to be dismantled.

Education has to move beyond the confines of the conventional curriculum with its emphasis on reading, writing and arithmetic. Education must now include the mastering of knowledge by *all* people *regardless of gender* in the areas of science, engineering, technology, computers and communication. There is also a need for a thorough examination of the curriculum to ensure that it does not continue to promote neo-colonial values and attitudes that mystify reality and sustain the economic, political and cultural domination of Africa. In view of the continuing crisis in Africa, education should now be used as a tool of liberation that will enable people to understand the root causes of their oppression and act in concerted ways to end it.

It would be useful at this juncture to examine two social and ecological situations in which the majority of African women's activities are concentrated, namely agriculture in the rural areas and trade in the urban areas. These represent two of the areas of greatest vulnerability in terms of the general marginalization of women within the context of retrogressive development.

Rural Women and Agriculture

The majority of sub-Saharan African women (the estimate is about 70-90 per cent), live in rural areas and often outnumber men in countries such as Swaziland, Kenya and Lesotho. In all rural economies in Africa women play vital economic roles such as farmers, food processors, livestock tenders, house repairers, food collectors, handicraft manufacturers, traders, housewives, health care providers, cultural transmitters and socialization agents. Because of the multiple nature of their roles, most women in rural areas are overworked and have limited time for participating in political activities. Many are uneducated and illiterate, have no knowledge of their legal and political rights and are generally unaffected by international events such as the UN Decade for Women.

Women play an important role in agricultural production world-wide but the role of women in sub-Saharan African agriculture is paramount. According to the FAO the female labour force in agriculture ranges from 30-50 per cent and in food production it can be as high as 90 per cent in some areas. The intensive involvement of women in food and cash crop cultivation appears in a variety of roles ranging from unpaid family worker to independent cash crop farmer. A number of socio-economic and demographic factors such as marriage instability and male migration are resulting in an increasing number of households headed by women. It is also customary as a result of the widespread practice of resource-based usufruct land use for women to have access to land under traditional law.

Despite the recommendations and programmes of the Decade many African women continue to face several constraints that are related to socio-economic factors operating at the international and national levels, and which restrict access to land, credit, technology, imports, training and information. Changes in land use and land tenure patterns, whereby more land is allocated to cash crop production at the expense of food crop production and where privatization of land severely restricts access to communal land, can have devastating effects on women. Social disruptions caused by divorce, separation, death or migration of a husband can render women landless, resulting in their migration to other areas and seeking employment as farm labourers or becoming destitute (UN, 1986). A study of 1,696 farmers in the Brong Ahafo region of Ghana found that as many as 70 per cent of women who lost their land as a result of one or more of the reasons stated above sought employment as farm labourers (Andah, 1978).

Access to resources such as land, technology, finance, imports, and so on, continues to be a problem for many women farmers and is likely to get worse given the limitations imposed by the financial crisis facing most African countries. Despite the fact that there is evidence of women's willingness to reinvest a proportion of their incomes derived from cash crop farming, they often have difficulty obtaining loans and increasing their farm size.

Related to this are constraints faced by women in terms of lack of contact with extension workers who are still predominantly male. Poor marketing infrastructure, inadequate transportation, and lack of government commitment to small farmers could also impose serious constraints on women. In some cases, as in a district in Zambia, women farmers have been known to refuse to produce crops in the absence of a good marketing infrastructure. Much still needs to be done in terms of improving rural economies, especially in the reduction of past harvest losses and in the establishment and maintenance of food security, afforestation schemes and public facilities. In view of the food and water crisis in many parts of Africa, special attention will have to be given to emergency and relief measures to prevent massive human suffering.

Women also play a critical role in subsistence forestry, which is not often recognized. Subsistence forestry utilizes trees and tree products for food, fuel, building materials, tools, handicrafts, medicines, dyes and fodder for household use. Over 300 million people who practice swidden agriculture (shifting cultivation) on nearly 50 per cent of the land in the tropics depend on women as the primary participants in subsistence forestry. In Africa women are the major collectors and users of fuel wood and because of their familiarity with the forests, are usually more knowledgeable about plant species, resources and the products of forests. According to one study, foresters have had to learn a lot from women through discovering the sound and environmentally safe forestry management practices used by women in developing countries. For example, customary rules governing fuel collection often encourage the collection of dead and drowned wood and prohibit the cutting down of viable living trees (Fortmann, 1986). In view of their vested interest in forestry conservation, women have often taken preventive measures to forestall the negative consequences of development projects related to forestry, as is evidenced in a case in Mali. Implementers of a soil and water conservation project in Mali discovered that local women had already undertaken conservation efforts that would have been destroyed by the project (ibid.).

Nevertheless, many forestry projects in Africa have been undertaken without the recognition that women are the local forest experts, managers and labourers. Despite the primary role of women in subsistence forestry a study of 43 World Bank forestry projects found that only eight made specific reference to women (Scot, 1980). As one study notes:

The presumption that it is only men who are involved in forestry is totally wrong. . . .In part this state of affairs is due to the masculine images conjured up in the word forestry. The reality is, in fact, often the opposite of the image...women have traditionally played important roles in agricultural production and in the use and management of trees. (Fortmann and Rocheleau, 1985)

Some rural economies have been decimated by natural disasters and women are disproportionately affected by such calamities. The consequences of drought, whether in the Sahel or Ethiopia, include food deficits, water shortages, destruction of livestock, shortage of fuel and rural to urban migration. These combined factors have contributed to increasing women's workload in rural areas. According to one report:

The drought has brought on an abandonment of the land by men who have migrated towards the urban centers in search of work. This migration, whether permanent or temporary, has increased the responsibilities of the women in helping to maintain the family's economic equilibrium. This responsibility leads the women to be much more active than is traditional, both at home and in the field. (Sakona et al., 1986)

Women's critical and central roles in food systems and in the interrelation of problems concerning food, fuel and water have received some rhetorical recognition but do not yet constitute an essential and viable part of policy and planning activities. To neglect strengthening women's work as producers, providers, managers in artisanal subsistence economics is to sound a death-knell to any development plan.

As a result of the influence of priorities at the international level many African countries continue to ignore sound and scientifically based indigenous theories and practices of environmental conservation and farming practices used by

African women for centuries. Furthermore, the inimical nature of development has now created a situation in which millions of people in Africa are unable to have their basic requirements for physical well-being met.

Because of the general deterioration of rural economies, resulting primarily from retrogressive development, a number of women are migrating to urban areas or have husbands and family members who have migrated to the cities. Consequently there are linkages between the urban and rural areas that have important demographic implications as well as ensuring the flow of food and other resources through networks of social relations. It is virtually impossible, in thinking of social development, not to recognize this rural-urban connection that may provide some useful approaches to reversing the trend towards rapid and premature urbanization through excessive rural to urban migration. An approach that focuses on the more dynamic population group in this rural-urban continuum may be more effective in promoting rural development rather than one that locates all operations exclusively in the rural area.

Urban Women and Trade

Urbanization has been regarded as the most important social transformation in modern times. While in 1800, only 3 per cent of the world's population lived in cities, by the turn of the present century the world's urban population will be four times what it was in 1950, with most of the increase taking place in cities of the Third World. In the year 2000 urban dwellers will outnumber the rural population for the first time in the whole of human history (Sachs, 1986). Although Africa is the least urbanized region of the world, its cities are growing the fastest and so are the numbers of its urban poor. Urban facilities and services as well as food, energy and housing are often inadequate. Unemployment is rife, slum conditions prevail and for the majority, the standard of living is well below poverty levels. Since migration is not the result of urban labour demands stemming from industrialization, most African cities are consumer cities rather than producer cities.

Migration to the cities often has a coercive element that is related to the deteriorating conditions of many rural economies. Women are either left behind to provide for their families with diminishing resources or migrate themselves with or without their families. Female rural to urban migration has been increasing and in Ethiopia and Tanzania have surpassed male migration (Richie).

The typical profile of the migrant woman is as follows: young, illiterate, unskilled for urban employment and unfamiliar with urban norms. Many live in slum dwellings, have children and eke out a living in the informal labour market as traders, artisans, food processors, maids or prostitutes. Marriage and family ties tend to be tenuous in such environments and serial concubinage is more common. Marriage instability as well as desertion often results in a high percentage of female-headed households living well below subsistence levels. Usually there is a breakdown of traditional patterns of co-operation so that many of these women face conditions of social and cultural isolation as they struggle to support their families and raise their children against insurmountable odds.

It has been estimated by the ILO that between 20 and 70 per cent of the labour force in Third World cities make a living in the informal sector. With an average of over 50 per cent of poor urban populations so engaged, the informal sector occupies approximately one in eight of the world's adult population. This is regarded as an important and valuable sector that is nonetheless vulnerable and often occupied largely by migrants who are unable to make a living on the land, or unable to find a formal job in the city. Individually, the majority of such people can barely subsist on their earnings and often have to pool their resources with kinfolk or through new associations in the city. Despite these realities, the informal sector itself is believed to generate around a third of the wealth of many cities in the developing world.

In Africa, as stated earlier, the rural and urban areas represent not two distinct spheres but *closely connected and integral economic domains*. There is a dynamic link that is maintained not only by the kinship ties between urban and rural folk, frequent travel and a certain degree of return migration, but also by a dynamic network of trade and reciprocal obligations that ensure the constant flow of human and material resources.

Trade within the informal labour market context is a major occupation for women and in some countries in West Africa accounts for about 90 per cent of the female labour force. Nevertheless, women often face several constraints as a result of poor market infrastructure, inadequate transportation services, lack of essential skills and education, difficulties in obtaining licences, poor storage facilities, inadequate security and lack of access to credit. Many women traders in addition work under strenuous conditions that can be hazardous to their health. Women traders in urban areas also face structural constraints resulting from world-wide economic changes and recessionary trends. Within the internal marketing system women's trading activities are often at the level of subsistence or on the lower ranks of the trading hierarchy. According to the World Survey on the Role of Women in Development (UN, 1986), women traders do not represent a homogeneous group but widely varying socio-economic groups, which is reflected in the nature of their trading activities. The first category, representing the majority of female urban traders, consists of subsistence traders who are engaged in the retail trade of agricultural surpluses, processed foods, local handicrafts and small household items. This is a highly time-consuming, high-risk and low-profit operation engaged in by the most vulnerable urban population who are often illiterate and unskilled. There is an element of instability in this type of trading activity and return migration or frequent travel to the rural home towns are not uncommon.

The second category comprises women traders who retail or market wholesale quantities of farm and marine products. These women play a strategic role in the economy because they regulate the major part of the food supply to urban areas, manage sizeable amounts of capital and travel extensively in order to carry on their full-time activities as traders (Boserup, 1970). Some of these women have become quite wealthy.

The third group of women traders sell a wide variety of products ranging from foodstuffs to expensive jewelry in retail and wholesale quantities. Although they are in the minority, their social impact can be significant, since some have become successful as businesswomen and community leaders.

Despite the success of a small minority of women traders, the majority barely make a living above subsistence and operate under unfavourable social, economic and personal conditions.

> Since trader's organizations often exert a certain control in various ways of traders engaged in the marketing of popular goods the incoming illiterate traders are for the most part pushed into trade in the informal sector, such as street-side stalls or itinerant trade around the streets and in suburban markets where the competition is even stiffer. The growing size of cities increases the traders' burdens, the cost of urban transport, the mobility required and the cost of storage facilities. These obstacles mean loss of revenue and smaller or no profits for most of these traders. (UN, 1986)

In addition women traders are often confronted with changes in consumer demands, expansion of male commercial activities that can result in trading alliances with other men at the expense of women traders. Competition from supermarkets and contract trade present additional obstacles to women. Women traders are also subject to harassment by the police in countries where they are considered a nuisance and can be used as scapegoats during periods of political unrest. In keeping with the nature of the development process in many African countries, government policies tend to provide assistance, support and security for big private and public enterprises at the expense of the small female trader (ibid.).

For some urban women, prostitution provides the only means of livelihood and represents a growing trend during conditions of economic crisis. Like trade and other activities in the informal sector, prostitution is not a lucrative economic activity for most women who earn wages that are barely above subsistence level. The social implications of prostitution in the context of retrogressive development can have far-reaching consequences in terms of threatening the social fabric and well-being of whole nations.

Urbanization is yet another example of retrogressive development within the context of dependency. In Africa, most urban centres have historically been functional cities for moving produce and minerals overseas and for maintaining the administration of such activities. In this regard, the current process of urbanization is not conducive to Africa's development. Urban centres also reinforce inequalities on the basis of race, class and gender and thus foster social discontent. Many of the problems of social development are best exemplified in the decaying social fabric that characterizes many cities in Africa. Women have become marginalized through the process of urbanization and represent the worst form of wastage of human resources and potentials. 'In many senses, wastage of human potentialities for work is by far the worst form of wastefulness, the more so in that opportunities foregone are lost forever - human lives cannot be stocked for later use' (Sachs, 1986).

Towards Positive Development for African Women

Instead of generating more strategies and 'lists of wishful thinking' that go by the name of recommendations or resolutions at the international level, the approach to the African social crisis could proceed along the following lines:

1. *Reduction of external involvement*

Within the context of dependency, no one can really expect solutions to come from the very structures that benefit from Africa's retrogressive development. Consequently one important line of action is to significantly reduce and arrest the negative obstructive and counterproductive influence on womens' lives by several externally oriented international organizations, aid agencies, research institutions and non-governmental organizations. Many reflect the dominating and exploitative character of north-south relations in terms of upholding dependency and providing justifications for its continuation.

The Decade and its aftermath have witnessed the emergence of a large number of institutions, programmes, activities and research projects in industrialized countries on the complex question of women in development. The assumption that problems can be solved through the proliferation of foreign 'experts' as well as foreign-controlled 'women's projects' and 'research activities' has proven to be false.

The main preoccupation of many of these ventures, which is the generation of fancy reports for consumption elsewhere, has had little or no impact. In fact, some of these groups serve to maintain the imperialistic hegemony of the north - this time with the help of women. Meanwhile several regional institutions with outstanding records for advancing the social conditions of African women, such as the African Training and Research Center for Women (ATRCW) and the Association of African Women for Research and Development (AAWORD), operate under continuous resource constraints. Donor agencies would rather give substantial financial support to northern-controlled institutions in keeping with the nature of dependency.

In some instances externally oriented research activities can serve as an imperialistic tool to facilitate domination, since these research projects seldom investigate the fundamental issue of the unequal nature of international economic relations. The negative impact of many externally oriented projects on women and other groups is also often ignored.

External economic and cultural domination also establishes priorities on the basis of outside interests. For example, the interest in the sexuality and fertility of African women continues to be given top priority by northern establishments at the expense of more urgent problems of economic exploitation and oppression brought about by northern-controlled policies and practices. While many African countries and women's groups in Africa are working towards the elimination of injurious practices such as female circumcision, the obsession with this issue in the north is often presented with racist overtones. International women's groups have been formed in northern cities such as London, Geneva and Boston that address the issue of female circumcision in Africa while black, Indian and other women of colour are subject to violence, involuntary sterilization and racial oppression in some of these countries.

Wives of African ambassadors have sometimes been recruited to serve in prominent roles in a number of these associations. How much more profound and effective it would have been if these groups, some of which represent the northern elite, lobbied the governments and economic establishments to end the exploitation and oppression of African women through their unjust economic policies. Additionally, they could devote much time and effort to ending their government's support for the racist apartheid regime in South Africa as well as take on the noble cause of eliminating the oppression of women there.

Racism has played an important role in the exploitation of the African continent and no solution to the serious African social situation must overlook that important fact. The link between racism and capitalism expressed and institutionalized through imperialistic relations continues with virulent zeal in current world economic relations. As Africans we cannot afford to forget that the world economic system is intrinsically racist both in its mode and in its operation. The best and most succinct articulation of the link between racism and capitalism in relation to Africa was made by Nkrumah:

> Each historical situation develops its own dynamics. The close links between class and race developed alongside capitalist exploitation. Slavery, the master-servant relationship and cheap labor were basic to it. The classic example is South Africa where Africans experience a double exploitation - both on grounds of color and class. (Nkrumah, 1975)

One fundamental and essential prerequisite for reverting the African social situation is liberation from the shackles of neo-colonial domination in the political, economic, social, cultural and personal spheres of African peoples' lives. This is even more important for poor women who are often disproportionately affected by the consequences of retrogressive development and experience multiple forms of exploitation and oppression.

2. *Promoting Internal Development*

Solutions have to come from within Africa. The Lagos Plan of Action provided a framework for self-reliant development that influenced the Arusha Strategies for the Advancement of African Women. Given the protracted nature of dependency, retrogressive development and the current economic and social crisis in most of Africa, the implementation of these strategies present a supreme challenge for the regional and national institutions and African non-governmental organizations.

A triple approach aimed at the elimination of dependency, poverty and gender inequality seems inevitable, since all these conditions are intricately linked. As the social conditions of many African countries worsen, the value of women as essential human resources for survival increases. Consequently women must not be marginalized in any realistic plan for Africa's recovery.

Social transformation is essential and must take place at the political, legal, economic, social, cultural and personal levels, since the development, well-being and happiness of all people must be the primary outcome of any development process.

At the political level, there is a need for wise and enlightened use of power equally distributed between men and women so that people-centred development can take place. This would require mass mobilization of men and women in political movements for change. Another equally important political dimension concerns the need to drastically reduce military spending and divert these resources to activities that will benefit women. Above all, African leaders have to be more accountable to the people and responsive to the needs and concerns of women.

At the legal level, solutions have to be long-term with lasting effects, backed by resources and monitoring efforts. Long-term solutions must involve the destruction and transformation of structures that have maintained the subordination of women.

At the economic level there is a need for a fundamental change that would focus on internal development rather than export-oriented agricultural and industrial development that undermine social development.

At the social level, urban and rural groups should be mobilized that use traditional mechanisms for participation and activism to prevent further deterioration in the African social situation and to promote positive social development. In addition, emergency action will be needed to arrest the suffering of masses of African people, particularly women, children, the aged, the sick and the disabled.

At the personal level, African women must be provided with an environment that promotes a sense of social worth, dignity and happiness and ensures their safety at all times. Development of the full potential of each woman and promotion of a sense of personal satisfaction and well-being must be given top priority by society and by women themselves.

3. *Culture as a Mechanism for Social Development*

In order to forestall the retrogressive trends in Africa's social situation and promote some of the worthy and still viable objectives of the Lagos Plan of Action, culture has to be understood and used as a tool of mobilization, participation, production, reproduction and resistance. In this regard the role of women as custodians and transmitters of cultural traditions will be paramount.

For centuries, African societies sustained self-reliant and viable economies that ensured the physical, cultural and social well-being of large communities, cities and states. This was made possible in part by culture, the collective elements of a group that provide a design for living through language, knowledge, beliefs, art, material objects, technology, music, dance, and so on. Individuals acquire cultural attributes as members of society through a process of socialization in which a key role is played by the mother.

The integration of African societies into the world economic system destroyed many aspects of African culture that promoted social and use values and replaced them with individual and exhange values more conducive to the norms of the market and often detrimental to women. For example, natural resources such as land, trees, the sea, etc., were resource based and owned collectively by the community. Rights of usufruct ensured access to members of the community and both labour and distribution of the products of labour were organized to ensure that no member of the community would ever be in need. The old, infirm, disabled and very young were cared for, as well as the widowed, divorced and single members of society. Traditional mechanisms for dispute settlement minimized conflicts between men and women and women's traditional societies served as mechanisms for the promotion of women's rights. The welfare of the community, whether it functioned as a lineage, clan or tribe was paramount. All efforts, cultural norms, attitudes, behaviour, institutions and social organizations were geared towards the maintenance and promotion of the interests of the corporate group. Although all was not perfect, this was social development at its best!

Externally oriented values, lifestyles and patterns of consumption that stress consumerism, individualism, social inequality and exploitation of the weak can undermine social development unless vigilant and concerted efforts are made to prevent it. A traditional process of socialization in which a key role is played by the norms of social development and responsibility and in which cultural values are preserved can be compatible with market forces, if development does not take place within the context of dependency. The example of Japan provides concrete evidence for this.

African countries can begin to reverse the negative trends in development by retrieving and reviving some of the positive aspects of African cultures that stress social development and value human beings above material objects. In many of these cultural norms women were valued for their roles in society and the female symbol represented the ideal principle that sustained all life. For example, women's role in agriculture is not simply an economic variable but a socially valuable principle. There is a collective element in most African cultures that links women symbolically with land productivity and for which women traditionally received much respect. Their role in reproduction was intricately linked to fertility and the nurturing of human beings and hence of the group. In effect it was the role of women that ensured continuity of the group. The female principle thus became equated with life-giving and life-maintaining forces as well as with the promotion of social well-being and welfare, which are central elements in African development. Africa has within its boundaries some of the best elements for social development that are not only rooted in its past but have become the only relevant and viable options for the positive and self-reliant development of the future.

Africa is probably the continent that has suffered most in terms of the way in which gender subordination became linked with other forms of social, political and economic oppression through the colonial and post-colonial experiences. It is therefore the only continent likely to be in a position to make the greatest contribution to the world by promoting real and effective conditions for gender equality and the genuine advancement of women.

References

Amin, S. (1974), *Accumulation on a World Scale*, New York: Monthly Review Press.

Amin, S. (1974), *Modern Migration in Africa*, London: Oxford University Press.

Amin, S. (1974), *Neo-Colonialism in West Africa*, New York: Monthly Review Press.

Andah, K. (1978), 'Ghanaian Women in Agriculture. The Case of Food Production', paper presented at seminar on Women in Development, University of Ghana, September 4-8.

Boserup, Esther (1970), *Women's Role in Economic Development*, New York: St Martin's Press.

Clairmont, F. and Cavagagh, J. (1987), 'The World Debt Crisis Threatens a Collapse in World Trade', in *Ifda Dossier*, 59, May/June.

Copenhagen Programme of Action (1980).

Da Gama Santos, M. (1985), 'The Impact of Tourism on Women in Developing Countries', *Journal für Entwicklungs Politic* (JEP), 4.

D'Onofrio-Flores, P. (1982), 'Technology, Economic Development, and the Division of Labor by Sex', in P. D'Onofrio-Flores and S. M. Pfafflin, *Scientific-Technological Change and the Role of Women in Development*, Boulder, Colorado: Westview Press.

Dos Santos, T. (1968), 'El nuevo caracter de la dependencia'

(Santiago) *Cuadernos de Estudios Socio-Economicos*, 100, Centro de Estudios Socio-Economicos, Universidad de Chile.

ECA (1985), Preparatory Meetings for the Nairobi Conference, Arusha.

F.A.O. (1988), *Food Outlook*.

Fortmann, L. and Rocheleau, D. (1985), 'Women and Agroforestry: Four Myths and Three Case Studies', *ICRAF*, April.

Fortmann, L. P. (1986), 'Women in Subsistence Forestry', *International Forestry*, 84, 7, July.

McFadden, P. (1982), 'Female Employment in the Food Industry in Swaziland', paper presented at the Dag Hammarskjold AAWORD Seminar, Dakar.

Moorehouse, W. (1979), 'Science, Technology, Autonomy and Dependence: A Framework for International Debate', *Alternatives*, IV, 3, January.

Ngalwa, T. (1974), 'Domestic Labor and Property Ownership, A Case Study of Hubangwa Village in Mwanza District', unpublished ms.

Nkrumah, K. (1975), *Class Struggle in Africa*, New York: International Publishers.

Richie, J. 'The Integration of Women in Agrarian Reform and Rural Development in English Speaking Countries of Africa', ARR/CS/e5.

Sachs, I. (1986), 'Improving Life in the City', Work in Progress, UNU, 10, 1, October.

Sakona, Y. et al. (1986), 'Women: Food and Energy Providers of the Sahel', Work in Progress, UNU, 10, 1, October.

Scot, G. (1980), *Forestry Projects and Women*, Washington DC: World Bank.

Sen, G. and Crown, K. (1987), *Development, Crises, and Alternative Visions: Third World Women's Perspectives*, New York: Monthly Review Press.

Sivard, R. (1985), *World Military and Social Expenditures*, Washington, DC: World Priorities.

Steady, F. C. (1982), 'African Women, Industrialization and Another Development', *Development Dialogue*.

Steady, F. C. (1987), 'Pan African Women, Science and Technology', paper presented at FESPAC pre-festival, Dakar, Senegal, December.

Traove, A. (1982), 'Agro-Business and Female Employment in the

Ivory Coast', paper presented at AAWORD conference 'Women in RuralDevelopment', Algiers.

UN (1985), *Review and Appraisal of the UN Decade for Women.*

UN (1985), *State of the World's Women.*

UN (1986), *World Survey of the Role of Women in Development.*

UNEP (1985) African Environment Conference, December. Department of the Executive Director of the United Nations Environment Program. (Prepared in conjunction with the OAU and ECA).

Vasques de Miranda, L., 'Women's Labor Force Participation in a Developing Country: The Case of Brazil', Wellesley Editorial Committee (eds), *Women in Development: The Complexities of Change.*

7 Demographic Factors, Labour Supply and Employment in Africa

Seyoum G. Selassie

Sub-Saharan African populations are, perhaps, the fastest growing populations in the world, while the region is now seriously affected by socio-economic crises unknown anywhere else in the last quarter of the present century.

The Lagos Plan of Action, which was adopted as an agenda for action to begin the reversal of downward trends in development, did not produce the desired results, mainly because of the inability of member states to harmonize policies and development programmes to advance the goal of collective self-reliance - the Lagos Plan's corner-stone.

Economic and social problems assumed critical proportions in the early to the mid-1980s, mainly as a result of unfavourable world commodity market situations and adverse climatic conditions. It must also be said that unabating civil strife within countries and international conflicts have contributed a great deal to the worsening of socio-economic conditions in the region.

Africa's rich natural resource potential is the equal of those of the other major regions of the world. It is estimated that Africa has 97 per cent of the world reserves of chrome, 85 per cent of platinum, 64 per cent of manganese, 25 per cent of uranium, and 13 per cent of copper and other mineral resources (OAU, 1981).

Opinions vary concerning the factors perpetuating the continuing state of underdevelopment in the region, and indeed the precipitous worsening of this situation in the last two decades. According to Unicef the roots of the problem are:

1 The anti-agriculture and hence anti-rural bias in development policy, resulting in a widening developmental gap between the urban and rural sectors.
2 The increasing dependency of the region on imported food.
3 The inability and unwillingness of policy-makers to create domestic capacity for generating needed factor inputs (i.e., the almost total absence of research and development efforts designed to develop technologies appropriate for the region's needs).
4 Unabated population growth, which places heavy demands on ill-developed resources and continuously threatening the delicate population-resource balance (1985).

The purpose here is not to engage in the debate on the mix of determinants of African underdevelopment, but to isolate employment as an element in the set of development indicators and show how this element relates to factors such as population growth-rates and growth-rates in the labour supply, the carrying capacity of the economic system and its likely consequences for labour productivity and community welfare.

Among the consequences of the population growth-rate for labour productivity, welfare levels, and hence for socio-economic development are:

1 The young age structure of the population and its consequences for the population-resource balance.
2 The unbalanced relationship between the increase in the size of the labour force and such measures of the degree of development as GDP growth-rate.

3 Increasingly skewed income distribution among different socio-economic groups.

The Demographic Situation

Many underdeveloped countries are currently experiencing a 'demographic transition' of the type that was experienced by the new industrialized countries during the early 1900s. This transition represents a secular trend in declining fertility following considerable declines in mortality in response to fundamental economic and social transformation. However, the rapid rate at which populations in sub-Saharan Africa are growing is a consequence of a fairly rapid decline in mortality while fertility has remained high. All the available evidence points to the fact that sub-Saharan Africa is still in the first stage of demographic transition.

The data indicate that there was only a slight decrease in the crude birth-rate from 1965 to 1985. The average crude birth-rate in 1965 was 47.2 per 1,000 population and this decreased slightly to 45.6 per 1,000 in 1985. On the other hand, the average crude death-rate of 22.1 per 1,000 population in 1965 fell to 16.1 per 1,000 in 1985. There was also a substantial reduction in the region's child mortality rate between 1965 and 1985. In 1965 the child mortality rate, (i.e., mortality among children aged one to four years) was 35.4 per 1,000 population. This decreased to 20.5 per 1,000 in 1985. The overall fall in crude death-rate, combined with relatively constant levels of fertility, has lead to a more rapid population growth, while improved survivorship as a result of the lowered child mortality rate has led not only to an increase in the demand for formal education, but also to an increase in the demand for work that will probably be sustained in the near future.

For the region as a whole the population increased at the rate of 2.7 per cent annually between 1965 and 1980 and at the rate of 2.9 per cent between 1980 and 1985. If fertility remains at the present high rate (45.6 per 1,000 in 1985) the region's population is expected to grow at the rate of 3 per cent between 1985 and the year 2000. In about 20 countries the population growth-rate had already exceeded this figure between 1980 and 1985, when rates were reported at between 3.0 per cent and 4.1 per cent. The highest reported growth-rate in the period 1980-1985 was that for Kenya (4.1 per cent) and the lowest was for Mauritius (1.3 per cent).

Population Growth, Age Structure and Age Dependency

One of the effects of rapid population growth is some decline in the proportion of the population that is of working age (i.e., between 15 and 64 years). For the region as a whole, the working-age population decreased from 52.4 per cent of the total population in 1965 to 50.9 per cent in 1985. This can be attributed to the consistently high fertility rate during the period, giving rise to a younger age profile for the total population, which means in turn that the age dependency burden has increased, if only slightly. Nevertheless, This slight increase in the age dependency burden is likely to have detrimental effects on the already low level of labour productivity in the region.

Fourteen out of the 40 countries for which data are reported are likely to face more problems related to increased dependency burdens and hence declining labour productivity. At the same time there are a few countries where the size of the working-age population relative to the size of the total population has remained almost constant or even increased. Examples of the latter are Rwanda, Sierra Leone, Mauritania and most notably Mauritius.

Population Growth and Structural Differentiation in Economic Activity

A good measure of the degree of structural differentiation of the economy and economic activity is labour force distribution among the major economic sectors. A comparison of the sectoral distribution of the labour force in 1965 and 1985 shows that, on the average, the percentage of the total labour force in agriculture fell from 77.5 per cent in 1965 to 69.1 per cent in 1985. During the same period the percentages of the total labour force in industry increased from 7.3 per cent to 10.4 per cent. The service sector accounted for 12.7 per cent of the total labour force in 1965 and 18.7 per cent in 1985. These averages hide considerable variations within the region and especially among the sub-regions. Generally the North African sub-region leads in the degree of structural differentiation of economic activity. The exceptions in sub-Saharan Africa are Ghana and Mauritius.

Two other useful measures of the degree of structural differentiation in the economy are the sectoral origins of Gross Domestic Product (GDP) and its sector-specific growth-rates. We can characterize the position of sub-Saharan Africa relative to other developing regions of the world with different resource endowments, and with the industrialized market economies. In the developing countries as a whole between 1965 and 1986, there has been a marked decline in the contribution of agriculture to GDP (from 29 per cent to 18 per cent), and a slow rise in the contribution of industry (from 29 per cent to 34 per cent). In sub-Saharan Africa there was a significant decline in the share of agriculture in GDP - from 39 per cent in 1965 to 31 per cent in 1973, followed by a declining trend to 35 per cent in 1986. In the early to mid-1980s, however, the movement was more erratic. On the average, agriculture represented 32 per cent of GDP from 1980 to 1986, and industry contributed 28 per cent. For the developing countries generally agriculture represented 19 per cent of GDP from 1980 through 1986 and industry 35 per cent. Clearly the degree of structural differentiation in the economy in the Africa region is much lower than in many of the developing regions, and sub-Saharan Africa has remained dependent on agriculture.

In the oil-exporting developing countries, the agricultural contribution to GDP declined fairly consistently from

22 per cent in 1965 to 14 per cent in 1980 and to 17 per cent in 1985 and 1986, while the contribution of industry rose from 29 per cent to 35 per cent. For the high-income oil exporters, agriculture contributed 4 per cent of GDP and industry 54 per cent in 1965, and 2 per cent and 56 per cent, respectively, in 1986. A similar situation pertains for the industrialized market economies, where agriculture contributed 5 per cent of GDP and industry 40 per cent in 1965, and 3 per cent and 36 per cent, respectively, in 1986.

Sector-specific growth-rates declined steadily from the early 1970s to the mid-1980s. From an average annual growth-rate of 2.7 per cent from 1965 to 1973 agriculture-based GDP decreased to 0.4 per cent between 1973 and 1980 and to 0.9 per cent between 1980 and 1985.

Industrial growth was quite significant from 1965 to 1973 (13.8 per cent). However, this decreased to 4.1 per cent during 1973-80 with a negative growth of -2.3 per cent between 1980 and 1985. The growth-rate in the service sector also declined from 5.1 per cent in 1965-73 until a negative growth of -0.4 per cent was recorded for the period between 1980 and 1985.

These figures show that sub-Saharan economic systems had reached the limits of their population-carrying capacity in the early 1970s. Among the many factors producing this state of affairs are rapid population growth, stagnant technology, the international commodity market situation and development policy biased against agriculture. The contribution of rapid population growth is considerable because person/resource ratios tend to increase unless they are offset by rapid technological development. Excessive population pressure on land and other resources reduces productivity unless an effective means of diverting this pressure is found through measures to stimulate structural differentiation of the economy.

Attempts to develop the urban economy through accelerated industrialization are also frustrated by the lack of capacity to generate domestic factor inputs and the rela-

tively low level of effective demand for industrially produced goods. The decline in food production that characterizes the current African economic scene undermines the
material base for industrial development. This maintains the
vicious circle of rural underdevelopment that militates against
the development of a viable industrial sector, and this in turn
perpetuates rural underdevelopment.

The Problem of Urbanization

Theoretically, the degree of urbanization can be used as an
estimate of the degree of structural differentiation of economy and society. In the African situation, however, such an
interpretation of urbanization must be made with caution.
Even though the percentage of total urban population in
Africa has increased since the 1950s, it cannot be said that
this growth has been matched by commensurate development in economic and social infrastructure. This reservation
is supported by the fact that the shares of industry and
services in GDP have decreased since the early 1970s.

Urban populations in the various sub-regions have
increased at different rates. In the North African sub-region
44.3 per cent of the total population were living in urban
areas in 1980. This figure is expected to reach nearly 52 per
cent in 1990 and 59 per cent by the year 2000.

The second most urbanized sub-region is Central Africa
with 34.5 per cent of the population living in towns and cities
in 1980. The projections for 1990 and the year 2000 are 44 per
cent and 52 per cent, respectively.

Urban growth in West Africa is more moderate. In
1980 only 22.5 per cent of the total population lived in urban
areas and this is expected to increase to 29 per cent in 1990
and 36 per cent in the year 2000.

The East African sub-region is characterized by a
remarkable heterogeneity in terms of the rate of urban
growth. There are a few countries like Mauritius and Malawi
where in excess of 60 per cent of the total populations live in

urban areas, and others like Burundi and Rwanda with less than 5 per cent of the total population living in urban areas in 1980. Generally, Eastern Africa has the lowest urbanization ratio - 16.4 per cent in 1980, with a projected increase to 23 per cent in 1990 and 29.6 per cent in the year 2000.

Of the three countries in the Southern African sub-region for which data are reported, Botswana has the largest proportion of population living in urban areas - 29.5 per cent in 1980, and this is expected to increase to nearly 53 per cent in 1990 and 63 per cent by the turn of the century. Lesotho and Swaziland are predominantly rural with only 4.5 per cent and 8.9 per cent of their respective populations living in urban areas in 1980, and an expected 10.7 per cent and 15.9 per cent by the turn of the century.

A few conclusions may be drawn from this outline of urbanization in the Africa region.

1 Since a significant component of urban population growth is the result of migration, such a growth is likely to be spontaneous rather than planned. It is more than likely that this spontaneous growth will put considerable demands on the carrying capacity of the socio-economic and political environment.
2 Since migrants are generally without skills that will enable them to operate effectively in a modern economy, they are likely to remain in a marginal status, playing roles that are disruptive to rational socio-economic behaviour. This often manifests itself in the form of increased crime rates, prostitution and other forms of anti-social behaviour.
3 Even when employed, new arrivals to the urban labour market tend to depress the level of productivity.

Employment Growth in Africa in the 1970s and Early 1980s

Since independence, the state in Africa has been the dominant agency for leading rapid socio-economic development. This has customarily been effected through periodic plans in which major problems are identified, priorities set, resources mobilized and shares of the different sectors of the economy specified. The stated goals in such plans include an increase in the general and sector-specific output of goods and serv- ices, raising the standard of living of the population and diversifying employment opportunities. The purpose here is not to discuss the merits of development planning but rather to look at efforts to achieve these worthwhile goals through the mobilization of available human resources by creating more employment opportunities. Trends in em- ployment growth in Africa between 1975 and 1983 do not show any consistent pattern. In 1975 the mean annual growth-rate was 3.9 per cent, and 6.4 per cent at the end of the decade after three years of erratic movement. The pres- ent decade opened with a growth-rate of 3.4 per cent, which increased to 6.5 per cent in 1981 and declined to a negative rate of -3.9 per cent in 1983 - a reduction in overall measur- able employment. This suggests that the employment situ- ation in Africa is unpredictable at best. Furthermore, there are indications that the share of wage employment in total employment has been quite low.

In 1980, the year for which data are available, wage workers represented only 12.8 per cent of the total labour force in sub-Saharan Africa. The lowest proportion of total labour force in waged employment is that reported for Niger (1 per cent) and the highest for Mauritius (60.5 per cent - an exceptionally high wage employment rate). Twenty of the 34 countries in the region, or 58.8 per cent, have wage employ- ment rates of less than 10 per cent of the total labour force (Benin, Burkina Faso, Burundi, Cameroon, Ethiopia, Guinea, Lesotho, Madagascar, Mali, Mauritania, Mozambique, Niger, Rwanda, Senegal, Sierra Leone, Somalia, Tanzania, Togo, Uganda and Zaire); eight countries or 23.5 per cent have wage employment rates of between 10 per cent and 20 per cent (Congo, Ivory Coast, Ghana, Kenya, Liberia, Malawi, Nigeria and Sudan); 8.8 per cent have wage employment rates of between 20 per cent and 30 per cent (Botswana,

Gabon, Zambia); only 5.9 per cent of countries have wage employment rates of between 30 per cent and 40 per cent (Swaziland and Zimbabwe).

Clearly, the majority of workers outside the wage employment sector are those in traditional agriculture. It is also reasonable to assume that, of workers in the non-agricultural sector, the majority are likely to be in the informal sector.

Per Caput GDP as a Measure of Labour Productivity

Admittedly labour is not the only determinent of the degree of wealth accumulation. Domestic production relations, resource endowment and international economic relations are also important factors. Nevertheless, the capacity of countries to develop and utilize human resources effectively stands out as an important determinant of productivity. The rapid rate of population growth in the Africa region has frustrated attempts at striking a balance between population and resources, with the consequence that both standard of living and productivity have declined.

A comparison of population and GDP growth-rates per caput for sub-Saharan Africa, other developing regions, and the industrialized countries reveals the following picture. The growth-rates in GDP for the developing countries generally, with a total population of 3,123 million in 1980, were rather erratic. Practically no growth in GDP was recorded for 1982 and 1983 and fluctuating improvement for 1984-6 (3.1, 2.7 and 2.5 per cent). For sub-Saharan Africa (1980 population 331 million) the picture was even more gloomy. During the period 1982-6 the region experienced negative growth in GDP per caput (-4.3, -4.9, -4.8, -0.2, and -2.3 per cent in sequential years). Even the oil-exporting developing countries, with a total population of 405 million (1980) experienced negative growth in GDP per caput over the 1982-6 period (-3.6, -4.5, 0, -0.2, and -3.2 per cent). Exporters of manufactures (population 1,886 million in 1980) fared better, with GDP growth-rates of 2.1, 3.3, 6.2, 6.1, and 5.4 per cent 1982-6, while the industrialized market economies (716 million population in 1980) recorded mean annual growth rates in GDP per caput of -1.3, 1.6, 4.1, 2.4, and 1.9 per cent over the same period.

The situation is indicative of declining system and worker productivity that in at least one sense contributed to the imbalance between population growth-rates and resources.

Welfare Levels

The level of welfare of a population may be measured in a number of ways. For the purpose here we use the pattern of income distribution, accessibility and adequacy of health services, and nutritional status. The accessibility and adequacy of such resources as health services and nutrition are associated with the capacity of society to generate resources, and this in turn is, at least in part, determined by the productivity of available human resources. The level of welfare in turn affects the level of system and worker productivity.

Income Distribution

The pattern of income distribution is a function of the socio-economic status of the population. Reliable income distribution data are notoriously hard to obtain in the Africa region, and for that matter in many of the countries in the underdeveloped regions. Using limited data available for five countries - Kenya and Zambia (1976), Egypt (1974), Mauritius (1980/81), and Ivory Coast (1985/86), we can form a very rough general picture of the pattern of income distribution. One cannot assert with any degree of certainty that the situation in countries without reported data is different from those for which some data are available.

In the countries mentioned above, the poorer segments of the population, which represent 80% of the total population, share a small proportion of total income: about 40% of total income in the case of Ivory Coast, Kenya, Mauritius and Zambia, and 52% in the case of Egypt. The most recent data available (for Ivory Coast, 1985/86) show that the lowest 20 per cent of the population command only 2.4 per cent of total income while the highest 20 per cent command 61.4 per cent. Similar inequalities exist in Kenya, Zambia and Mauritius as well, and Egypt departs from this pattern only as a matter of degree, with the lowest 20 per cent of the population commanding 5.8 per cent of total income in 1974, and the highest 20 per cent commanding 48 per cent.

One probable explanatory factor is the high risk of both unemployment and underemployment among people of lower socio-economic status. Since wage levels are also generally low and the age dependency burden is high, both household income and individual income are generally low. The pattern of income distribution is also a measure of worker productivity. It is reasonable to argue that a combination of demographic factors such as a young population profile, inegalitarian social policy and international economic relations combine to produce the pattern of income distribution obtaining in Africa today. It is also reasonable to conclude that this pattern of income distribution impedes the participation of people in the development effort and perpetuates the state of underdevelopment.

Health and Nutritional Statuses of the Population in Africa

The ability of workers to produce goods and services to meet both basic and higher needs is partly determined by their health and general physical and psychological fitness. The following general picture emerges of the health and nutritional statuses of populations in the entire region. Ratios of physician to population decreased from 1 doctor to 29,538 people in 1965, to 1 to 21,381 in 1981. The nursing personnel to population ratio changed from 1 nurse to 5,753 people in

1965, to 1 for every 2,284 in 1981. These ratios hide considerable inter-country variations. For example, in 1965, the
physician to population ratio varied from 1 doctor per 2,300
people in Egypt to 1 per 74,000 in Burkina Faso. In 1981,
physician to population ratios varied between 1 doctor per
760 people in Egypt to 1 per 88,000 in Ethiopia. Similar
variations are observed in the nursing personnel to population ratios.

The mean nutritional status of populations in the region was low in 1965 and continues to be low in 1985. The
daily calorie intake per caput amounted to an average of
2,117 calories in 1965 and increased very slightly to 2,182
calories in 1985. This is perhaps less than 75 per cent of the
required daily calorie intake. This means that the average
African worker has less energy-giving food available than is
required for effective physical work - a fact that must contribute to the low productivity of labour in the region.

Summary and Conclusions

We have outlined the relationship between demographic
factors such as the rate of natural population increase, the
age structure, labour supply and productivity, as well as the
likely relationship between demographic factors, employment and income distribution. Although income distribution data were available for only a few countries, it is possible
to surmise that there is a high degree of income inequality
throughout the continent. This may, in part, be explained by
the fact that people's access to national wealth is limited by
high rates of unemployment and underemployment.

Employment is a means of enabling people to be at
once agents and beneficiaries of economic development,
while health levels and nutritional status are important
determinants of productivity. These factors are reflected, if
only indirectly, in the negative growth in GDP per caput
recorded for the region as a whole in the 1980s. While there
is very little that African governments can do to improve the

situation, they can reduce the impediments to the effective development and utilization of human resources by adopting policies to reduce the population growth-rate.

Notes

Diejomaoh, V. P. (1985), 'Employment Situation Prospects in Africa', paper presented at the Inter-Parliamentary Conference on Employment in Africa, Dakar, October (mimeo.)

ILO, *Year Book of Labour Statistics*, various years.

OAU (1981), *Lagos Plan of Action for the Development of Africa 1980-2000*, Addis Ababa,.

United Nations Children's Fund (1985), *Within Human Reach - A Future for Africa's Children*, New York.

World Bank (1987), *World Development Report*, New York: Oxford University Press.

List of Contributors

Adebayo Adedeji: Professor of economics; he is UN Under-Secretary-General, Executive Secretary of the UN Economic Commission for Africa, and Chair of the ACARTSOD Governing Board. He has initiated many measures aimed at the economic and social development of the African continent.

Barbara E. Harrell-Bond: The Director of the Refugee Studies Programme, University of Oxford, Dr Harrell-Bond is the author of numerous publications on Africa, and on involuntary migration in particular, including *Imposing Aid: Emergency Assistance to Refugees* (Oxford: OUP, 1986).

Austin N. Isamah: Dr Isamah obtained a Ph.D. in sociology at his home University of Ibadan in 1984, and is currently Senior Research Fellow, ACARTSOD. He has published a number of articles on wage employment, employee participation and the Nigerian Labour Movement, as well as trade unionism in Cameroon.

Eric P. Kibuka: Professor and Head of Department of Sociology and Social Work and Administration at Makerere University, Kampala, Uganda. His research concerns are issues of social work, social administration and social policy, and he has published extensively in the field.

Ali A. Mazrui: Professor of politics; currently at the Centre for Afro-American and African Studies, University of Michigan, Ann Arbor, USA. Among his many publications are *Towards a Pax Africana* (1967); *Violence and Thought* (1969), *The Trial of Christopher Okigbo* (1971), *Cultural Engineering and Nation Building in East Africa* (1972); co-ed.: *Africa's International Relations* (1978), *Nationalism and New States in Africa* (1984).

Seyoum G. Selassie: Professor of Sociology, University of Addis
Ababa, Ethiopia, has researched and written on social development generally and youth unemployment in Ethiopia, and has
worked as consultant and adviser on social issues and social
policy to regional and international organisations and agencies.

Filomina Chioma Steady: Co-Ordinator/Director, Women's Studies Program, School of Arts and Social Sciences, California
State University, Sacramento, USA. Born in Sierra Leone.